THE

INQUISITION

THE QUEST FOR ABSOLUTE RELIGIOUS POWER

By Kenneth Bartolotta

Portions of this book originally appeared in *The Inquisition* by Don Nardo.

LUCENT

PRESS

Published in 2017 by
Lucent Press, an Imprint of Greenhaven Publishing, LLC
353 3rd Avenue
Suite 255
New York, NY 10010

Designer: Deanna Paternostro
Editor: Siyavush Saidian

Cataloging-in-Publication Data

Names: Bartolotta, Kenneth.
Title: The Inquisition: the quest for absolute religious power / Kenneth Bartolotta.
Description: New York : Lucent Press, 2017. | Series: World history | Includes index.
Identifiers: ISBN 9781534560499 (library bound) | ISBN 9781534560505 (ebook)
Subjects: LCSH: Inquisition–Spain–Juvenile literature. | Spain–Church history–Juvenile literature.
Classification: LCC BX1735.B36 2017 | DDC 272'.20946–dc23

Printed in the United States of America

CPSIA compliance information: Batch #CW17KL: For further information contact Greenhaven Publishing LLC, New York, New York at 1-844-317-7404.

Please visit our website, www.greenhavenpublishing.com. For a free color catalog of all our high-quality books, call toll free 1-844-317-7404 or fax 1-844-317-7405.

contents

Foreword

History books are often filled with names and dates—words and numbers for students to memorize for a test and forget once they move on to another class. However, what history books should be filled with are great stories, because the history of our world is filled with great stories. Love, death, violence, heroism, and betrayal are not just themes found in novels and movie scripts. They are often the driving forces behind major historical events.

When told in a compelling way, fact is often far more interesting—and sometimes far more unbelievable—than fiction. World history is filled with more drama than the best television shows, and all of it really happened. As readers discover the incredible truth behind the triumphs and tragedies that have impacted the world since ancient times, they also come to understand that everything is connected. Historical events do not exist in a vacuum. The stories that shaped world history continue to shape the present and will undoubtedly shape the future.

The titles in this series aim to provide readers with a comprehensive understanding of pivotal events in world history. They are written with a focus on providing readers with multiple perspectives to help them develop an appreciation for the complexity of the study of history. There is no set lens through which history must be viewed, and these titles encourage readers to analyze different viewpoints to understand why a historical figure acted the way they did or why a contemporary scholar wrote what they did about a historical event. In this way, readers are able to sharpen their critical thinking skills and apply those skills in their history classes. Readers are aided in this pursuit by formally documented quotations and annotated bibliographies, which encourage further research and debate.

Many of these quotations come from carefully selected primary sources, including diaries, public records, and contemporary research and writings. These valuable primary sources help readers hear the voices of those who directly experienced historical events, as well as the voices of biographers and historians who provide a unique perspective on familiar topics. Their voices all help history come alive in a vibrant way.

As students read the titles in this series, they are provided with clear context in the form of maps, timelines, and informative text. These elements give them the basic facts they need to fully appreciate the high drama that is history.

The study of history is difficult at times—not because of all the information that needs to be memorized, but because of the challenging questions it asks us. How could something as horrible as the Holocaust happen? Why would religious leaders use torture during the Inquisition? Why does ISIS have so many followers? The information presented in each title gives readers the tools they need to confront these questions and participate in the debates they inspire.

As we pore over the stories of events and eras that changed the world, we come to understand a simple truth: No one can escape being a part of history. We are not bystanders; we are active participants in the stories that are being created now and will be written about in history books decades and even centuries from now. The titles in this series help readers gain a deeper appreciation for history and a stronger understanding of the connection between the stories of the past and the stories they are a part of right now.

1095–1099 . . . . 1233 . . . . 1431 . . . . 1478 1492

The Inquisition arrests, tries, and executes the French warrior-maiden Joan of Arc.

Years of the First Crusade, in which European nobles and others lead armies to Palestine to take the region from Muslims.

Jews are expelled from Spain; the last Muslim stronghold in Spain is conquered.

Spain's King Ferdinand and Queen Isabella establish the Spanish Inquisition.

Pope Gregory IX establishes the medieval Inquisition.

| 1542 | 1543 | 1600 | 1633 | 1966 |

Pope Paul III establishes the Roman Inquisition to protect the Catholic Church from Protestantism and other so-called heresies.

The trial of Galileo Galilei by the Roman Inquisition begins.

The Roman Inquisition burns scientist Giordano Bruno at the stake for challenging the scientific beliefs of the Church.

Polish astronomer Nicolaus Copernicus publishes his famous book, *On the Revolutions of the Heavenly Spheres*, which advocates the heliocentric view of the universe.

The Catholic Church abolishes its index of banned books, begun by the Roman Inquisition in the 16th century.

CONTEMPORARY VIEWS ON THE INQUISITION

In simple terms, the Inquisition was a series of trials and punishments instituted by the Catholic Church beginning in medieval Europe. However, the history of the Inquisition is far from simple. For starters, there was no single Inquisition: there were many different individual inquisitions held throughout Europe over a number of centuries. These took place in different areas, targeted different minority groups, and their motivations were both religious and political.

Though there were numerous reasons for each Inquisition, the main goal was to seek out and ultimately eradicate any individual who challenged the beliefs and rituals of the Catholic Church. Individuals who disobeyed the traditions and rules of the Church were referred to as heretics.

The first Inquisition started in the early 1200s and is commonly known as the medieval or papal Inquisition. The Inquisition began in France, but over time, it spread to other countries and across Europe. The goal of this Inquisition was to deal with heretics, most notably Joan of Arc, the French warrior-maiden who was eventually burned at the stake.

The initial Inquisition was followed two centuries later by the Spanish Inquisition. Widely known as the most famous Inquisition, it was designed to rid Spain of anyone not Catholic, specifically targeting Jews and Muslims. Though it originated in Spain, the Spanish Inquisition also spread to portions of both North and South America.

The last Inquisition created by the Catholic Church was the Roman Inquisition. This Inquisition is historically remembered as targeting modern science and the thinkers

In this painting, King Ferdinand and Queen Isabella hear the pleas of a Spanish Jew during the Spanish Inquisition.

Sorting Out the Violence of the Inquisition

Learning about the activities and events of the Inquisition involves some distasteful, disturbing, and even frightening images. This is partly because of the intolerance of the inquisitors (the men in charge of searching for heretics and putting them on trial). Anyone who dared to think or worship in ways that deviated from Catholic traditions was subject to arrest and trial. These trials were not fair, impartial proceedings like those in modern democracies. Instead, in an Inquisition trial, the accused was presumed to be guilty from the start and forced to confess their guilt—even if they were innocent. The tactics employed to obtain these confessions were often brutal and inhumane. Over the centuries, thousands of people underwent horrendous tortures and many suffered agonizing deaths, often being burned alive. Indeed, the

whose ideas challenged church doctrine. The most notable and famous of these thinkers was Italian astronomer Galileo Galilei.

Some Inquisitions were religiously motivated, some politically, and some both. Regardless of purpose, however, because each one was sponsored by the Catholic Church and used similar methods, it has become common in modern times to collectively refer to these series of trials as the Inquisition.

Inquisition has come to be closely associated with the concepts of intolerance, injustice, torture, and murder.

However, was the Inquisition any more intolerant than other medieval institutions? Were the inquisitors the only authority figures in Europe who conducted torture and grisly executions? A number of historians and other modern observers are quick to point out that they were not. Because historians have the ability to look back at the context of these Inquisitions—the societies, cultures, and practices surrounding them—it is easy to see that they are a product of their environments. Although considered corrupt and brutal by today's standards, their actions were not at all unusual for their time. As scholars Michael Baigent and Richard Leigh wrote:

The Inquisition was the product of a brutal, insensitive, and ignorant world. Not surprisingly, it was itself in consequence brutal, insensitive, and ignorant. It was no more so, however, than numerous other institutions of its time ... Many of the ... worst [cruelties] were caused by individuals acting with what,

The Inquisition used numerous forms of torture. This drawing depicts a stretching rack.

according to the knowledge and morality of their time, they deemed the best and worthiest of intentions. We would be rash to imagine our own worthy intentions as being infallible.[1]

Edward Peters of the University of Pennsylvania, a noted scholar of the Inquisition, agreed. He pointed out that when the Inquisition began to search for heretics, severe criminal laws were already in place and torture was commonly practiced in Europe's secular (nonreligious) courts. "A good deal of Inquisition history," Peters wrote, "has been written as if the papal inquisitors were the only ardent pursuers of alleged wrongdoers in 13th-century Europe. In fact, they were always less numerous, and often less ardent than the judicial servants of secular powers."[2]

Indeed, secular authorities and courts in medieval Europe routinely used methods and punishments such as torture and burning at the stake. Moreover, the secular authorities often persecuted the same groups that the Catholic inquisitors did. For example, Jews, Muslims, and Protestants, all major victims of the Inquisition, were also frequent targets of soldiers and prosecutors for political reasons or because of simple hatred. Furthermore, the Inquisition prospered during an age in which women and children were routinely abused by husbands and fathers, people believed in witches and thought that demons could take possession of people's bodies, and slavery was considered perfectly ethical and supported by God.

Protestant Interpretations of the Inquisition

Despite its roots of conflict and violence, some of the Inquisition's bad reputation may not be totally deserved. Peters and another major modern scholar of the Inquisition, Henry Kamen, pointed out that many modern depictions of the Inquisitions exaggerate both their degree of organization and the number of victims they killed. This, they say, is largely because of propaganda spread by Protestant writers from the 1500s well into the 1800s. These were the years in which Protestant religions separated from the Catholic Church, which was an action that left bitterness on both sides. Many Protestant denominations sought to distance themselves from Catholic ideas and rituals.

Thus, perhaps not surprisingly, the goal of many Protestant writers was to discredit the Catholic Church in as many ways as possible. Such propaganda depicted the Inquisition as a large arm or department of the Catholic Church that existed as a single, powerful unit for seven centuries. That church department, Protestant writers wrote, was supposedly designed to deprive them and other non-Catholics of their liberty. As Kamen wrote: "Protestant pens depicted the struggle of heretics as one for freedom from a tyrannical faith. Wherever Catholicism triumphed, they claimed, not only religious but also civil liberty was extinguished."[3]

Yet only during some periods was the Inquisition a formal, well-organized department within the Church. Often, tribunals intended to root out heretics were set up in various countries on an as-needed basis. Each was a separate, mainly local, institution that was unrelated to the others. Moreover, sometimes the church and its leader, the pope, had little or no direct control over the inquisitors. In the case of the Spanish Inquisition, for example, most of the inquisitors worked directly for and took their orders from Spain's king and queen, sometimes to the frustration of the popes in Rome.

The horrors of the Spanish Inquisition are another case in which the facts were later distorted. This inquisition was used by the rulers of various European countries to disparage and discredit Spain. This is because these rulers and their countries often viewed Spain as their political, economic, and military enemy. The common charge was that Spaniards were a barbaric, inferior people because they and their corrupt rulers had conducted the Spanish Inquisition. In his 1581 tract, the *Apologia*, for instance, the noted Dutch Protestant statesman William of Orange claimed that Spaniards were uncivilized and bloodthirsty. He cited "the brightness of the fires" of the Inquisition, "wherein they have tormented so many poor Christians."[4]

Thus was born the so-called Black Legend, which told of Spain as a land of cruel religious fanatics. Claims such as the following from a Puritan preacher were very common; he wrote that when French troops invaded Spain in 1808 during the Napoleonic Wars, they found secret torture chambers that had been used by the Spanish Inquisition:

Because of the Spanish Inquisition, William of Orange, pictured here, described the Spaniards as bloodthirsty barbarians.

Here they found the instruments of torture … The first instrument noticed was a machine by which the victim was confined and then, beginning with the fingers, all the joints in the hands, arms, and body were broken … until the sufferer died. [Another device was] a large doll, richly dressed and having the appearance of a beautiful woman, with her arms extended ready to embrace her victim … A spring caused the diabolical engine to open [and] its arms immediately clasped him, and a thousand knives cut him into as many pieces.[5]

Such descriptions were serious distortions of the truth. No such torture devices ever existed in Europe or anywhere else.

Unjust and Inhuman Practices

Yet the fact that there are so many myths about the Inquisitions must not be used as an excuse for their inhumane practices. Ample evidence shows that they and their agents did perpetrate what are now viewed as despicable acts. In an attempt to enforce religious conformity, they arrested people, confiscated their property, convicted them without fair trials, tortured them, and in some cases burned them at the stake or slowly drowned them to death. Even if these practices were commonplace in medieval European society as a whole,

they were still ignorant, brutal, and cruel. They are especially horrifying because they were sponsored by the Catholic Church.

Indeed, even modern Catholic authorities sometimes admit the reality of some of the Inquisition's abuses. One modern edition of the *Catholic Encyclopedia for School and Home* wrote of the Inquisition:

Historical evidence forces us to admit that on occasion inquisitors … committed grave crimes against justice, charity, and the human person by summarily condemning large numbers of heretics to death. The Inquisition not only offends modern ideals of justice and spiritual freedom, it also contradicts the teaching of the Fathers and Doctors of the Church, such as St. Bernard, who said: "Faith must be the result of conviction and should not be imposed by force."[6]

Still, the vast majority of scholars and other modern observers of the Inquisition agree that it should not be studied today for the purpose of passing judgment on the inquisitors. All reasonable people can agree that almost all of the methods the Inquisition used are uncivilized and inappropriate by modern standards. It is far more important to examine how the Inquisition came into being and what fueled its various manifestations over the centuries. It is also important to look at the victims of the Inquisition. How did their persecution, and in some cases their near or complete elimination from certain countries, affect the histories of those nations? Often, the Inquisition's victims were both people and ideas. This was the case when inquisitors went after Galileo and other thinkers who claimed that the sun, not Earth, was at the center of the universe. What effects did these attempts to slow, or even reverse, scientific progress have on science, society, and the Church itself?

In short, the ignorance and intolerance of the inquisitors and the terrible suffering they caused cannot be erased by condemning and dismissing them. Rather, it is important to try to understand them and their motives, so people today can better understand themselves and their own roots. An impartial examination of the Inquisition reveals some of the ways that, for good or bad, both religious faith and religious intolerance have helped to shape the modern world.

chapter one

THE BIRTH OF THE PAPAL INQUISITION

The 13th century was the start of the first Inquisition, commonly known as the medieval or papal Inquisition. It was a direct reaction by the Roman Catholic Church to those across Europe whose opinions and beliefs differed from those of the church. Leaders within the church were threatened by contradicting viewpoints, and considered anyone who voiced such opinions to be heretics. In order to silence them, they initiated the Inquisition.

The first victims of the Inquisition were a religious group known as the Cathars. Taking their name from the Greek word *katharos* (pure), Cathars lived mainly in southern France. Though they lived their lives based on the teachings of the Bible, they also held a number of beliefs that clashed with those of the Catholic Church. The Cathars preached the importance of simplicity and the need to abandon all luxury in one's life. In addition, and maybe most scandalous for the Catholic Church, was the central Cathar belief that Jesus was not divine.

These teachings, which directly challenged some of Christianity's core principles, drew the attention of Catholic leaders. This included Pope Innocent III. Innocent's reign as pope was one of the most powerful of the medieval period. In Innocent's eyes, the Cathars' very existence was a form of heresy. Quoted as calling the Cathars the "little foxes that spoil vines,"[7] Innocent felt that eradicating this group was necessary to maintain and protect Christian European society as well as the Catholic Church.

Innocent's attempts to eliminate the Cathars marks the beginning of the papal Inquisition. His belief in ridding Europe of such heretics would come to define all inquisitions that would follow.

The Church's Role in Medieval Society

People living in modern democracies, where freedom of religion is taken for granted, may find this medieval desire to destroy heresy a bit strange. Why did the popes and other medieval Catholic leaders feel so threatened? Simply because a few people wanted to worship in a different way? To understand why these church leaders felt threatened and why the Inquisition was created, one must first comprehend the crucial and often overpowering role the Church played in medieval society.

The Roman Catholic Church, which had developed during the last two centuries of the Roman Empire, became Europe's most powerful and influential institution after Rome fell late in the fifth century. In the centuries that followed, virtually every European who was not already a Christian became one, and people came to see the Church as a major guiding force in their lives. Even more than their country's rulers, the clergy, from

St. Peter's Square, pictured here, was the heart of Catholicism for centuries and drew huge crowds.

the popes in Rome to local parish priests, dictated what behavior was moral and acceptable to medieval Europeans. "All over Europe there was one church only," noted scholar Anne Fremantle wrote:

> If a man were not baptized into it, he was not a member of society. Anyone excommunicated [expelled from the Church] ... lost his political and legal rights as well ... It was the Church that insisted that the poor did not have to fast as much as the rich, and which forbade servile work on Sunday. It was the Church which provided the poor with social services—free food and hospitalization. There was, for a long while, no other source of education.[8]

The popes and other church leaders saw it as both their duty and their right to maintain a tight control of people's lives. They believed wholeheartedly that their God was the only one that existed and that their religion was the only legitimate one. All other gods and faiths were false, and the members of the Christian flock had to be protected from different religious beliefs and practices, or else they would be condemned to hell. On one hand, the authority figures in the church believed that allowing Europe

AN INQUISITOR'S ACCOUNT OF THE CATHARS

Bernard Gui, one of the inquisitors sent by the Catholic Church to France to root out heretics, described the Cathars this way:

> In the first place, they usually say of themselves that they are good Christians who do not swear, or lie, or speak evil of others; that they do not kill any man or animal, nor any thing having the breath of life, and that they hold [firm to] the faith of the Lord Jesus Christ ... They moreover talk to the laity [ordinary Christians] of the evil lives of ... prelates [high-placed clergymen] of the Roman Catholic Church ... Then they attack and vituperate [abuse], one after the other, all the sacraments of the Church, especially the sacrament of the Eucharist [Holy Communion], saying that it cannot contain the body of Christ ... Of Baptism, they assert that water is material and corruptible, and is therefore the creation of the Evil Power [Satan] and cannot sanctify the soul.[1]

1. Quoted in Leon Bernard and Theodore B. Hodges, eds., *Readings in European History*. New York, NY: Macmillan, 1958, pp. 141–142.

to be invaded by non-Christian ideas would go against the will of God; on the other, they were not willing to give up their immense power and control. Any deviation from established beliefs and rituals seemed to undermine the Church's authority. This simply could not be tolerated.

As a result, church leaders thought it was necessary to maintain the unquestioning devotion of all Christians. Most popes strove toward the goal of theocracy, a system in which the Church would have supreme authority over secular as well as spiritual affairs. Just like church leaders, however, the kings and nobles, though themselves devout Christians, were often reluctant to give their power up completely to the clergy. For centuries, popes and kings struggled over whose powers would be the greatest. Regardless, the Church had a great deal of success in controlling the masses of ordinary Christians throughout Europe. One way that it maintained such control was through fear.

In sermons, in written documents, and even in art, clergymen made it clear that people who did not adhere strictly to the traditional articles of the faith would be damned to hell. "Hell's torments were lovingly dwelt on and elaborated," scholar Louise Collins pointed out. "Every kind of roasting, screwing [twisting metal screws into the flesh], beating, boiling, disemboweling [cutting out the internal organs], was described in words, paint,

and sculpture."[9] Because the stakes were so high, disagreeing with church doctrines was seen not just as an honest difference of opinion. Rather, it was labeled heresy and viewed as a serious crime that threatened society, the Church, and God himself.

Saving the Souls of the Cathars

Thus, when Pope Innocent III launched his campaign against the Cathars, he truly believed that he was acting in the interest of God and the people making up his flock. The pope felt it was his solemn duty to maintain the integrity of God's established church and to save the souls of his fellow man—including those of the Cathars themselves. He reasoned that it was surely heresy to advocate, as the Cathars did, that Jesus was not divine; that the Church, its clergy, and its sacred sacraments (including marriage) were illegitimate and unneeded; that there was no such place as hell; and that after death some people were reincarnated as animals. By believing such things, Innocent felt, the Cathars were damning themselves in God's eyes. In addition, they were dangerous because they were constantly convincing traditional Catholics to join their heretical faith. This threatened not only the souls of the converted, but also the power of the Catholic Church.

Indeed, the Catharist community was rapidly growing in France. This was partly because of the seemingly virtuous manner in which most Cathars conducted themselves. They were pacifists (meaning they would not fight), and they claimed that they never lied or said anything bad against anyone else. Most importantly, they regularly preached that all people should model their lives after those of Jesus and his apostles, who had neither wealth nor an established church. Typical of a number of favorable descriptions of the Cathars from that era is this one by an anonymous observer:

The good Christians [the Cathars] have come into this land. They follow the path of Saint Peter, Saint Paul, and the other Apostles. They follow the Lord. They do not lie. They do not do to others what they would not have others do to them ... [The Cathars] are the only ones to walk in the ways of justice and truth ... Salvation is better achieved in the faith of these men called heretics than in any other faith.[10]

Seeing that more and more people regarded Catharism as an attractive alternative to traditional Catholicism, Pope Innocent III decided that he must try to stifle the Cathars. At first he employed mostly nonviolent means. For instance, he ordered the bishops who oversaw church affairs in the main areas where the Cathars lived to warn about the evils of Catharism in their sermons. The bishops also sent parish priests to reason with and hopefully re-convert Cathars to traditional Christianity. Because of the major role played by the bishops in these endeavors, the Church's early anti-Catharist campaigns are sometimes collectively called the Episcopal Inquisition (from *episkopos*, the Greek word for bishop).

Pope Innocent III launched a campaign against the Cathars, whom he considered heretics.

Resorting to Forceful Means

However, these largely peaceful efforts to quell the Cathars were unsuccessful, and the heretical movement

THE PRICE OF BURNING HERETICS

The inquisitors who ran the medieval Inquisition almost always kept detailed records of everything they did, including all the money they spent. The following is an accounting of the costs (in coins called sols and deniers) for burning four heretics on April 24, 1323, in France:

For large wood: 55 sols 6 deniers.

For vine-branches: 21 sols 3 deniers.

For straw: 2 sols 6 deniers.

For 4 stakes: 10 sols 9 deniers.

For ropes to tie the convicts: 4 sols 7 deniers.

For the executioners, each 20 sols: 80 sols.[1]

1. Quoted in Henry C. Lea, *A History of the Inquisition of the Middle Ages*. 4 vols. New York, NY: Harbor Press, 1955, vol. 1, p. 553.

continued to grow. In 1208, therefore, Pope Innocent III felt he had no choice but to resort to forceful means. The subsequent military campaign against the Cathars came to be called the Albigensian Crusade, named after the French town of Albi, one of the major strongholds of the Cathars. Answering the pope's call, thousands of knights, foot soldiers, and adventurers from all across Europe began to converge on southern France. Some were definitely motivated by feelings of duty to the pope and the Church. Others were convinced to join the crusade because Innocent promised that each participant would get a full pardon for any sins he had committed in his life. Still others were drawn solely by the prospect of collecting financial rewards, as all the property of the Cathars was to be confiscated and divided among the crusaders.

In the summer of 1209, an army of Christian crusaders and camp followers swept across southern France. One of the towns they singled out for attack was Béziers, because they had heard that Cathars lived there among the ordinary Catholics. The papal representative who accompanied these troops to act as their spiritual leader, Arnald Amaury, directed the crusaders to siege the city. Béziers had its walls breached in the space of only a few hours. What happened next is a matter that historians have still not settled.

One story says that just before the soldiers entered the town, one of the knights approached Amaury and asked how they would be able to distinguish the town's heretics from its devout Catholics. His cold-blooded answer has become one of the most infamous remarks in European history: "Kill them all," he said. "God will recognize his own."[11] Other reports claim that this is nothing more than a rumor that spread around the crusaders' camp. There is no debate, however, that the attackers then poured into Béziers and began massacring everyone; women, children, and Catholic clergy were killed along with the fighting men. Regardless of whether Amaury actually made that famous remark, it seems that the troops did indeed kill them all: an estimated 20,000 people were butchered. Of these, it is likely that only a few hundred were Cathars.

Following the slaughter at Béziers, the crusade dragged on slowly.

Because the Cathars were numerous and often hid from the crusaders, they were difficult to find and suppress. Pope Innocent realized that he needed to develop another weapon against the Cathars that could also be used against other heretics that might threaten the Church's authority. So he called on a group of friars to act as anti-heresy agents. Their job was to find and identify heretics and preach to them in an effort to convert them or sentence them to death if unsuccessful. The friars, who eventually came together into two formal orders—the Dominicans and Franciscans— made up the initial nucleus of what would soon become the medieval Inquisition.

The Dominicans formed around, and took their name from, one of Innocent's most trusted agents: Domingo de Guzman, now known as Saint Dominic. He began as one of the clergymen who accompanied the soldiers of the Albigensian Crusade. Even in the early stages of the crusade, he demonstrated that he was not afraid of using forceful methods against the Cathars and other heretics. At one point he made a speech that said in part:

I have sung words of sweetness to you [the Cathars] for many years now, preaching, imploring, weeping. But as the people of my country say, where blessing is to no avail, the stick will prevail. Now, we shall call forth against you ... and will

Officially Establishing the Inquisition

Under Pope Innocent III's successor, Honorius III, Dominic's followers were officially recognized as an order of friars. Although Dominic himself died in 1221, there were already about 200 Dominican friars in Europe. The next pope, Gregory IX, called upon this rapidly growing order to expand their activities against heretics. On April 20, 1233, Gregory issued a papal bull (decree) that told the local bishops:

We have ... determined to send preaching friars against the heretics of France and the adjoining provinces, and we beg, warn, and exhort you, ordering you ... to receive them kindly and treat them well, giving them in this ... aid, that they may fulfill their office [duty].[13]

The nature of that "office" became clear in a statement the pope issued directly to Dominicans just two days later: "[You] are empowered ... to proceed against them [the Cathars and other heretics] ... without appeal, calling in the aid of the secular arm [local non-church authorities] if necessary."[14] The friars were now official inquisitors and their mission, which steadily solidified into an institution, became known as the Inquisition. They now had the authority not only to hunt for and denounce heretics, but also to put them on trial and punish

Saint Dominic was a well-respected priest during the medieval Inquisition for both his holiness and his brutality.

cause many people to die by the sword, will ruin your towers, overthrow and destroy your walls, and reduce you all to servitude ... The force of the stick will prevail where sweetness and blessing have been able to accomplish nothing.[12]

Under Pope Gregory IX, the Church's efforts against heretics were expanded and magnified.

for the Dominicans—the *Domini canes*, Latin for "dogs of the Lord."

At first, there was considerable friction between these new inquisitors and local bishops. The bishops often felt that they were in competition with the inquisitors and that punishing heretics should be, as it had been before, the job of the bishops rather than special commissioners sent by the pope. In 1273 this dispute was finally resolved by Pope Gregory X when he ordered the inquisitors and bishops to work together and share authority in their efforts to eradicate heresy.

The Inquisition's Use of Torture

By this time, the Inquisition had developed a fairly standard set of methods. In most cases, a group of inquisitors suddenly appeared in a town and ordered all the inhabitants to meet in the town square. The chief inquisitor delivered a speech called the Edict of Grace. Essentially, he gave the citizens a grace period of 30 to 40 days, during which any and all heretics were urged to come forth and turn themselves in. If they admitted their sins, they would generally receive light punishment and be allowed to go free.

Otherwise, following the period of grace the inquisitors began to hunt down the "guilty." Suspected heretics were arrested and often tortured. Because it was widely viewed as unseemly for friars and other clergymen to shed

them. Some of the punishments were making it impossible to make wills or inherit property, the confiscation of property, and banishment for life. The next pope, Innocent IV, went a step further and allowed the inquisitors to turn condemned heretics over to the secular authorities for execution. (This was done because it was widely seen as wrong for a clergyman to take someone's life.) Innocent IV also officially allowed the use of torture during interrogations. Because of their increasingly brutal methods, a new name emerged

PREVIOUS EXAMPLES OF BRUTALITY

The friars and others who searched out, tried, and punished heretics during the medieval and other European Inquisitions were not the first legal or religious authorities to use torture in interrogations of prisoners or burn people at the stake. In fact, the medieval inquisitors most often merely continued using the same brutal methods that European society had inherited from the late Roman Empire. For centuries, torture was routinely used in Roman trials; at first it was mainly slaves who were tortured, but later free citizens suffered the same fate. Similarly, burning people alive was a common form of execution in Roman society. People who committed treason, patricide (killing one's father), arson, and sorcery were often burned at the stake. Also, during a long series of persecutions (which occurred before the Christians took charge of the Empire), Roman Christians were burned, an ironic foreshadowing of the burning of Christians by other Christians during the Inquisitions.

blood, the torturers generally avoided forms of torture that involved cutting or beating the victim. It became common, therefore, to cut off the victims' ability to breathe, stretch them on wooden racks, or force water down their throat until they choked. Methods "of this kind would seem to have been contrived to cause maximum pain and minimum mess,"[15] Baigent and Leigh remarked.

Not surprisingly, these and other gruesome tortures nearly always resulted in confessions, whether the person was guilty of heresy or not. After a confession the victim often received further punishment. This might include confiscation of property, banishment, or even death. However, some victims were allowed to go free if they named someone else as a heretic. Similarly, people who had confessed during the period of grace often escaped torture and serious punishment by naming names. Thus relatives, friends, and neighbors frequently informed on one another in hopes of saving themselves, which spread fear and undermined relationships of trust throughout society. "The Inquisition was ultimately interested in quantity," Baigent and Leigh wrote.

It was quite prepared to be lenient with one transgressor, even if he were guilty, provided it could cull a dozen or more others, even if they were innocent. As a result of this mentality, the population as a whole ... was kept in a state of sustained dread [that made

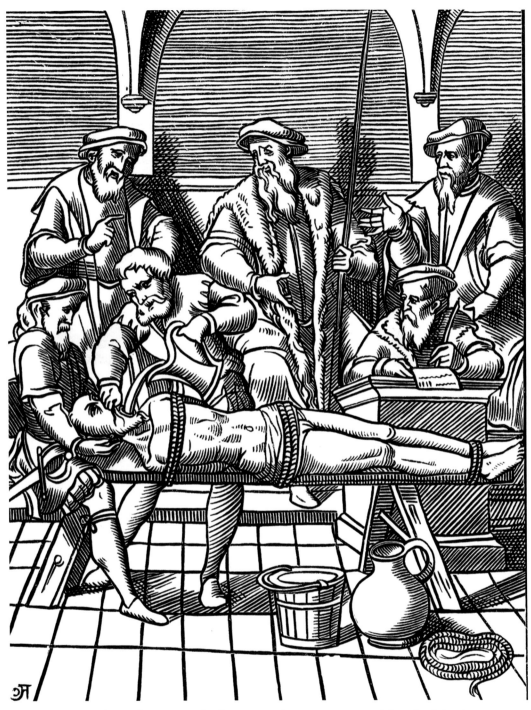

Water torture, shown here, was also known as the water cure and involved forcing water down someone's throat until he or she began choking.

them more vulnerable] to manipulation and control. And everyone, reluctantly or not, was turned into a spy.[16]

Those victims who would not inform on others or refused to admit their own guilt were subject to the worst penalties. In cases in which the inquisitors handed down a death sentence, it was time for the local secular authorities to get involved. When turning victims over to civil authorities, generally town officials or courts, the inquisitors recited words to this effect:

We dismiss you from our ecclesiastical forum and abandon you to the secular arm. But we strongly beseech the secular court to mitigate its sentence in such a way as to avoid bloodshed or danger of death.[17]

They delivered this statement with the full knowledge that the local authorities would not be willing to spare the accused. This efficient system of ecclesiastical tribunals, combined with continued military crusades, eventually achieved success in the effort to suppress Catharism. In 1244 the last major Cathar fortress fell, and in the next few decades the Inquisitional courts eliminated most of the remaining Cathars. (Some survivors fled to Italy while a few remained in France and continued to practice their rituals in secret.) Despite this success, the popes and their inquisitors did not feel that the threat of heresy was over. The medieval Inquisition remained in force for generations to come and claimed many more victims in the name of God.

CHAPTER TWO

THE POLITICS OF THE MEDIEVAL INQUISITION

The targets of the initial Inquisition varied. In the first 200 years, it was not just the Cathars whom the church viewed as heretics, but a number of other marginal groups that leaders felt it was necessary to prosecute. One of these other groups was the Waldensians. They were considered heretics because, among other reasons, they preached the word of God without the consent of the church.

In addition to the Waldensians, the Church also identified a small group of friars known as the Fraticelli as heretics. The Fraticelli are most known for speaking against the indulgence and greed of religious leaders. Even though they were members of the mainstream Catholic faith, any group that spoke against the Church was dangerous, and the Fraticelli were punished.

However, victims of the papal Inquisition were not just targeted for religious reasons. In addition, the Inquisition sought to eradicate its political foes. As a result, there was increased corruption within the Church. The clergy became divided between those who stuck firmly to Catholic ideals and those who did the bidding of influential monarchs throughout European society instead of obeying their religious superiors. This weakened the Church at all levels, and it is during this time that European kingdoms began to challenge the power of the papacy.

Throughout the medieval Inquisition, church leaders clashed with kings and queens. One notable example of this was Pope Boniface VIII, who refused to follow orders or directions from King Philip IV of France. Initially, Boniface excommunicated Philip, but the King refused to accept Boniface's order and retaliated by sending agents to kidnap him. They succeeded, and though the pope's capture was short-lived, the incident highlighted the vulnerability of religious leaders. Boniface died a month later, and this led to doubt and fear throughout the higher offices of the Church.

Following Boniface's death, the Church continued to weaken. In 1309, buckling under pressure from Philip and the French cardinals, the Church moved its headquarters from Rome to the French town of Avignon. The church would remain stationed in Avignon until 1378, the same year that two lines of popes emerged. One pope ruled in Rome and the other in France. A power struggle ensued that ultimately damaged the Church.

Now vulnerable, nonreligious leaders found it easy to take advantage of the Church and the Inquisition was exploited for political gain. Soon victims were targeted for strictly political instead of religious reasons. The two most notable victims of this time period were the Knights Templar and Joan of Arc.

Targeting the Waldensians

Long before Joan of Arc was born, when the popes were still widely viewed as strong and largely independent from the influence of secular rulers, the Church nonetheless faced the threat of heretical movements. The rise of Catharism in France in the late 1100s and early 1200s demonstrated that not all Christians in Europe held identical beliefs. Some followed the lead of a few charismatic dissenters. The leaders who established splinter groups had been born traditional Catholics, but at some time during their lives they had come to disagree with some of the Church's established ideas or rituals.

Among these dissenters was Peter Waldo, a successful and wealthy merchant who resided in the French town of Lyon. Around the year 1170, he underwent a major personal transformation.

Peter Waldo and his followers were a growing branch of Christianity before the Inquisition scattered them.

He decided that it was un-Christian of him to possess great wealth when there were so many poor people struggling to survive around him. So he gave away all of his money and became a beggar. Waldo also started preaching, and within a few years he had gained many followers. Many of his followers, so-called Waldensians, also felt a duty and calling to preach the word of God. To make their sermons more accessible to ordinary French peasants, Waldo had a local monk translate some parts of the Bible into French. (At the time, almost all versions of the Bible were in Latin and could be read and studied only by a relatively few educated people, mostly clergymen and noblemen.)

This created a problem for Waldo. The Church had strict rules that regulated both who could preach in God's name and who could distribute copies of the Bible. Only clergymen authorized by the papal offices or local bishops were supposed to be engaged in such activities. Ordinary people who had not been trained and ordained by the Catholic Church were forbidden from doing so. Peter Waldo tried to get the Church's permission to preach but was told to cease and desist. When he refused to comply, he was charged with contempt of ecclesiastical power. Other reasons the Church opposed Waldo and his followers included some listed in a document issued by Reinerius Saccho, a papal inquisitor, in 1254:

They despise all the statutes [laws] of the Church because they are heavy and numerous. [They also claim that] the Pope is the head of all errors ... that the Pope and all bishops are [murderers] on account of wars [such as the Crusades] ... that no one is greater than another in the church ... that no one ought to bow the knee before a priest ... that the clergy ought not to have possessions ... that the Bishops and Abbots ought not to have royal rights; that the land, and the people, are not to be divided into parts ... They condemn all the clergy for idleness, saying that they ought to work with their hands as the Apostles did.[18]

In addition, some of the Waldensian preachers were women, which was something the Catholic Church would not tolerate.

The Waldensians received numerous demands from popes, bishops, and other churchmen to give up their unacceptable beliefs and practices, but most of the followers continued to preach and worship as they pleased. So in 1215, the Church decreed that they were heretics, and some of the crusades launched against the Cathars also targeted the Waldensians. One problem the inquisitors encountered was that the Waldensians were more widely distributed than the Cathars. Waldo's followers eventually spread from France into Germany, Spain, Italy, Austria, Poland, and elsewhere,

THE STRANGE CASE OF THE BRETHREN

Among the many religious groups the medieval Inquisition persecuted was one known as the Brethren of the Free Spirit. They first appeared in the early 1100s in Italy, France, and Germany. Unlike the Cathars and Waldensians, whose views were still closely related to Catholicism, the Brethren were wildly unorthodox. They believed that all things, including humans, all animals, and even inanimate objects, were manifestations of God. Because all things were God, and God was good, all things must also be good. For them, this meant that every soul would be reunited with God after death. This was a direct contradiction of Church views, which stated that the only way to save one's soul was to be fully committed to pleasing God, which included going to weekly masses, confessing one's sins, and living a pure life. Telling people to abandon these traditions was a major threat to Catholic control. Even more troubling than this, the Brethren felt free to rape and steal, because they were unafraid of being condemned to hell. For these reasons, the Church condemned the Brethren and persecuted them with a vengeance. Hundreds of them were put on trial and killed, and the sect was mostly destroyed by the 1400s.

which made finding and prosecuting all of them impossible. The surviving Waldensians joined with other Protestants in their official split from Catholicism in the 1500s. Some descendants of the original Waldensians still exist in Europe and the United States.

The Church Persecutes the "Little Brothers"

Another religious group that Church leaders decided to rein in was an offshoot of the Franciscan order of friars. Founded in the early 1200s by the friar Francis of Assisi (later Saint Francis), the Franciscans had been among the friars chosen by Pope Innocent III to fight the Catharist heresy. What had impressed Innocent and other church leaders about the Franciscans was their devotion to core Christian principles. The order's friars dedicated themselves to public service, ministered to the poor, and were willing to work hard, day after day, with few material rewards. In the years following Francis's death in 1226, however, many Franciscans became more interested in acquiring wealth. Some came to live in fine houses, wear expensive clothes, and get involved in local political affairs. This was similar to the general trend among many clergymen around the same time, especially those in high positions. Certainly the popes and bishops lived in luxury and involved themselves in politics, often to the neglect of spiritual affairs.

However, some Franciscans were disgusted by this increasing materialism among clergymen, including members of their own order. One leading friar declared in 1257: "It is a foul and profane [unholy] lie to assert [the principle of] ... absolute poverty and then refuse to submit to the lack of anything, to beg abroad like a pauper and to roll in wealth at home."[19] As these two attitudes clashed, the order split into various factions in the late 1200s and early 1300s. Some stuck closely to the vows of poverty taken by their original founder and refused to indulge in any sort of luxury or worldly affairs, while others retained their comparatively extravagant lifestyles.

The popes and bishops did not like this turn of events. They worried about what the millions of regular people they controlled would think of the extreme contrast between the poor friars and wealthy churchmen. In 1317 they ordered the Franciscan splinter groups to join the mainstream of Franciscan and Dominican friars. One of these groups, whose members called themselves the Fraticelli, or "Little Brothers," refused. This prompted the Inquisition, now controlled mainly by the rival Dominican order, to swing into action. In the following year, four of the Fraticelli were arrested, convicted of heresy, and burned at the stake. More persecutions of the Fraticelli

Francis of Assisi established the Franciscan order, which was at first chosen by the Catholic Church to combat heresy but later considered a heretical group.

ensued, which distressed other Franciscans. In 1322, a group of mainstream Franciscans protested to the pope in writing and were shocked when he labeled their appeal to be heretical. The result was some two centuries of friction between the Franciscans and the Dominicans who ran the Inquisition. The inquisitors never attempted to go after the Franciscan order as a whole, but individual members of the

Fraticelli continued to be singled out for trial and punishment, and they gained a reputation as martyrs of the cause of ecclesiastical (spiritual) justice.

The Rise and Fall of the Knights Templar

In the charges the Inquisition brought against the Cathars, Waldensians, and Fraticelli, some sort of religious principles had been involved. However, this was not the case for all the targets of the Inquisition's tribunals. Some were singled out for political reasons and sometimes simply out of greed for money and power. The largest of these political persecutions was that of the Templar Knights (sometimes called the Knights Templar or just the Templars). Their organization had a unique combination of military and religious components. They were formed in the early 1100s, shortly after the capture of Jerusalem in Palestine by Christian armies in the First Crusade. In the years that followed, the Templars, who owed their allegiance to the popes, protected Christian pilgrims who journeyed to the Holy Land.

Over time, however, the Templars grew wealthy and increasingly independent of outside authority. By 1300, they had become the single most powerful institution in Europe besides the Catholic Church itself. Baigent and Leigh summed up the bases of their power:

The order owned immense estates across the whole of the Christian world ... The order owned ships, too ... The Templars commanded the most advanced military technology of the era. Their military resources ... exceeded those of any other European institution. They were also the chief bankers of Europe, adept at the transfer of funds throughout Christendom ... And they were widely respected diplomats, able to act independently of warring factions.[20]

The Knights Templar were created in order to protect Christian pilgrims and physically guard the Catholic faith.

Viewed as a threat to the Church, the Templar Knights were virtually eliminated through torture and execution between 1307 and 1314. In this picture they are burned at the stake.

These impressive assets and abilities of the Templars increasingly made them the targets of jealousy and hostility by various European monarchs and even by some of the popes. France's King Philip IV, who had managed to make Pope Clement V his puppet in the early 1300s, coveted the Templars' vast wealth and worried that they were planning to set up their own kingdom on French soil. In Philip's mind, the papacy and the Inquisition looked like the ideal tools to bring down the Templars, and he convinced Clement to issue the appropriate orders. In 1307, the Inquisition arrested all the Templars in France and seized their property. During the seven years that followed, many of the knights died either under torture or by execution. In 1314, the pope officially dissolved the Templars, although a number of them continued to live in various parts of Europe.

The Divine Mission of Joan of Arc

The Templars were not the only political victims of the medieval Inquisition. In the century that followed their persecution, France once again became the backdrop for the Inquisition's strictly political action. This time the victim was an individual rather than an organization. In the eyes of history, she was the single most famous person ever tried by the medieval Inquisition: her name was Jeanne d'Arc. Most people at the time referred to her as *la Pucelle*, "the Maid." Later generations came to call her Joan of Arc.

Joan was born in 1412 and later claimed that when she was 13 years old she began to hear the voices of the long-dead Christian saints Michael, Margaret, Gabriel, and Catherine. Joan sincerely believed that the voices came from God and that she had been given a divine mission to fulfill. That mission was to help the French nobleman Charles VII fight the English, who at the time occupied northern France during the Hundred Years' War. The young woman convinced Charles to give her leadership of a French army, and in 1429 she led that army to victory at Orléans and Patay. These victories were instrumental in holding back a full-strength English invasion of France, and other French successes followed. In May 1430 Joan was captured, however, and eventually ended up in the English prison at Rouen (in northern France).

The English feared Joan. This was partly because some thought she was a witch who could summon supernatural forces on the battlefield and partly because English leaders recognized that the Maid was a symbol of French nationalism. They thought she could still rally French armies against them. Simply killing Joan was not an option because she might become a martyr of the French troops, who would view her as a hero. So they endeavored first to discredit her popular image as someone doing God's will and make her look instead like a liar and a witch. The most effective way to do this, they reasoned, was to turn her over to the Inquisition.

Convicting and Executing Joan of Arc

Just like the other trials held by the Inquisition, Joan's featured no lawyers or juries. Several noted clergymen, called assessors, acted as advisors to the judges, who were inquisitors. The assessors were allowed to ask the suspect questions, but they had no authority to pass sentence. The chief judge was Pierre Cauchon, Bishop of Beauvais. He was also the leading inquisitor and prosecutor and did most of the questioning. In fact, the first stage of the trial, which lasted more than a month, consisted of repeated sessions in which Cauchon and other judges interrogated Joan.

As these sessions continued, the inquisitors did more than simply look for evidence that Joan was a heretic and witch. They also tried to discredit

SAINT MICHAEL WITHOUT CLOTHES?

The inquisitors who interrogated Joan of Arc took very detailed notes. Adapted from W.S. Scott's translation of *The Trial of Joan of Arc: Being the Verbatim Report of the Proceedings from the Orleans Manuscript*, the following dialogue shows Joan's resistance to the Inquisition:

> Inquisitor: *Of what form was Saint Michael when he appeared to you?*
> Joan: *I saw no crown on him; and of his clothes I know nothing.*
> Inquisitor: *Was he naked?*
> Joan: *Do you think that God cannot afford to clothe him?*
> Inquisitor: *Had he hair?*
> Joan: *Why should it have been cut off? …*
> Inquisitor: *Did Saint Michael and Saint Gabriel have natural heads?*
> Joan: *Yes, so I saw them. And I believe that it was they, as certainly as I believe that God exists.*
> Inquisitor: *Do you believe that God made them with heads as you saw them?*
> Joan: *I saw them with my own eyes. I will not say anything else.*

her in other ways, including calling into question her choice of attire. She wore men's clothes (because she was a soldier), and did so without shame. Though they repeatedly tried to get her to change into a dress, she stubbornly refused to do so. Typical was this exchange between Joan and a judge named Beaupère:

> Beaupère: *Will you wear [women's] clothes?*
> Joan: *Give me [some], I will take it and go away [leave prison a free woman]. Otherwise I will not take it. I am satisfied with what I have on since it pleases God that I wear it.*[21]

In the second phase of the trial, the inquisitors gave Joan a chance to save her soul. All she had to do, they said, was to admit her guilt and beg forgiveness from God and the Inquisition. However, she refused to be intimidated. She repeatedly claimed that her actions were the will of God, and she could not say that God's commands were heretical. So Cauchon proceeded to formally charge Joan with a number of offenses against God and the Church. To make the process look legitimate, he submitted the charges to a group of outside assessors, who were asked to give their opinions in writing. These men did not

DOUBTS OVER EXECUTING JOAN OF ARC

Years after Joan was executed, Isambart de la Pierre, an assessor at her trial, gave this testimony about the day of her death.

> One of the English, a soldier who particularly loathed Joan … was struck with a stupor or a kind of ecstasy when he … heard her crying on the name of Jesus in her last moments. He was taken to a tavern near the Vieux Marché to be restored to his senses with the aid of strong drink. And when he had eaten with a friar of the Dominican order, this Englishman confessed to the friar, who was an Englishman, that he had committed a grievous [terrible] sin, and that he repented of what he had done against Joan, whom he considered a saint. For it seemed to this Englishman that he had seen a white dove flying from the direction of France at the moment when she was giving up the ghost [dying]. And the executioner … that same day, came to the Dominican convent and said to me that he greatly feared he was damned, for he had burned a saint.[1]

1. Quoted in Wilfred T. Jewkes and Jerome B. Landfield, eds., *Joan of Arc: Fact, Legend, and Literature.* New York, NY: Harcourt, Brace and World, 1964, p. 79.

automatically approve of the charges as he had expected they would. Surprisingly, some of them suggested that the evidence was flimsy and that Joan might not be guilty of the charges. Though Cauchon would go on to ignore these objections and charge Joan with heresy, this incident demonstrates that the medieval Inquisition was not always simply a group of intolerant men conspiring to convict innocent people.

In the final stage of Joan's trial, inquisitors and guards took her to the cemetery of Rouen's Abbey of Saint-Ouen, where she was pronounced guilty. At this point she was offered one final chance to save her soul. She finally gave in, and signed a paper that admitted her guilt. The terms of this admission were simple: She admitted that her previous actions were wrong, and instead of death, she would be imprisoned for the rest of her life. There was only one additional condition—she must wear women's clothes.

Several days after this confession, she was found in her cell with men's clothes on. Moreover, she claimed that she had made a mistake in signing her confession. In the eyes of the Inquisition, she completely reversed any good will she had built up. Joan's judges and assessors met again, this time unanimously deciding to turn her over to secular authorities—the equivalent of a death sentence. Cauchon wasted little time in excommunicating her, and the execution that shortly followed was a public event. One eyewitness later recalled:

> She asked most fervently to be given a cross. And when an Englishman who was present heard this he made her a little one out of wood from the end of a stick, and handed it to her. She received it and kissed it most devotedly ... [Then] she was led off and tied to the stake [and burned]. Her last word, as she died, was a loud cry of "Jesus."[22]

Though the Inquisition managed to kill Joan, they ultimately failed to destroy her legacy. Just as English leaders had feared, the memory of her courage became a rallying cry for the French, who eventually drove the English completely out of France. Eventually, a special investigation launched by the Church found her trial to be filled with errors and fraud, and in 1456 her name was cleared. Finally, in 1920, the Catholic Church made Joan a saint. Many modern observers feel that her trial and brutal execution did more than any other incidents to permanently damage the reputation of the medieval Inquisition.

CHAPTER THREE

ROOTS AND OBJECTIVES OF THE SPANISH INQUISITION

Undoubtedly the most notorious inquisition was the Spanish Inquisition. Historians and other scholars do not look fondly upon the Spanish Inquisition for a number of reasons. The Inquisition is remembered for the cruelties it inflicted on both Jews and Muslims in the name of rooting out heresy in Spain and other countries. The Inquisition's details are gruesome, and much of its history is marked by torture, murder, and other elements of brutality.

The facts of the Spanish Inquisition are a topic of debate among scholars. While some historians cite a number of individual cases where murder and torture took place, other historians argue that much of the violence surrounding the Inquisition in Spain was exaggerated. In comparison to other Inquisitions that came before and after it, many scholars argue that

the Spanish Inquisition is no more or less cruel.

Brutality aside, there are a number of critical distinctions that separate the Spanish Inquisition from previous and later Inquisitions. Specifically, the Spanish Inquisition was not a product of the Catholic Church, nor its leaders, but instead was instituted by royal monarchs who ruled the country. The two main figures who presided over the Spanish Inquisition were King Ferdinand of the kingdom of Aragon and Queen Isabella of the kingdom of Castile. In 1469, the two monarchs joined forces when Ferdinand married Isabella, laying the groundwork for the later union of their kingdoms that resulted in the nation of Spain.

In addition to being separate from the Catholic Church, another difference was that the Spanish Inquisition

The Spanish Inquisition was created by Queen Isabella and King Ferdinand.

was less motivated by religion and more closely linked with sparking change on a national, political, and social level. Specifically, the Spanish Inquisition sought to identify and destroy different minority groups. Most notable of these groups were the Jews. The persecution of the Jews, and the attempts to convert them to Christianity, marks the beginning of the Inquisition in Spain. Their persecution was later followed by that of Muslims and different sects of Protestants. All of these groups were seen as a threat to Christian life in Spain during the time period.

The Origins of Anti-Semitism in Medieval Europe

To understand the motivations behind the Spanish Inquisition, one needs to examine the widespread anti-Semitism (hatred for Jews) in Spain and other European regions in that era. Deep-seated hatred for Jews in Europe was based in part on supposed crimes they had committed in ancient times. In particular, many Christians blamed all Jews, in all ages and places, for the death of Jesus Christ. (This irrational attitude was based on Christian belief that the Jewish authorities in Jerusalem had helped the Romans prosecute Jesus.) Jews also kept their traditional beliefs and rituals and refused to give them up. In a predominately Christian society, in which church leaders regularly preached that Christianity was the only true religion, this made Jews seem suspicious and potentially dangerous.

For these and other reasons, European Jews were often blamed for any crimes or problems in Christian communities, and various malicious myths developed that portrayed Jews as villains. One such myth claimed that Jews regularly kidnapped Christian children and butchered them in secret religious rituals. Whenever a Christian child was found dead of unknown causes, local Jews were the first suspects. Another common charge against the Jews was that they liked to steal the wafers that represent Christ's body in the Christian ceremony of Holy Communion. Jews supposedly pounded nails through the wafers with the evil goal of crucifying Jesus repeatedly.

Still another false accusation was that Jews often poisoned Christian wells and other water supplies in an effort to destroy Christian societies. The most hysterical charges of poisoning against Jews occurred during the onset of the bubonic plague (also called the Black Death), which spread across Europe from 1347 to 1351. Millions of people caught the disease and died horrible deaths. Despite the fact that many of those who suffered and died were Jews, most Christians readily believed the unfounded rumors that the natural disaster had been caused by Jews poisoning wells. An Italian observer wrote in April 1348:

Some wretched [Jewish] men were found in possession of certain powders, and (whether justly or unjustly, God knows) were accused of poisoning the wells—with the result that anxious men now refuse to drink water from wells. Many

This painting shows an allegory of the Jewish people being banished from Spain with the Edict of Expulsion.

were burnt for this and are being burnt daily, for it was ordered that they should be punished thus.[23]

Indeed, whether the charge was poisoning wells, stealing wafers, or kidnapping children, Jews were regularly persecuted throughout the medieval era. It was not uncommon for angry Christian mobs to attack Jewish communities, killing and maiming hundreds or thousands of innocent men, women, and children.

Jewish Prosperity and Growth in Spain

In spite of the rampant prejudice and random violence against Jews, Jewish communities enjoyed periods of prosperity and growth in some parts of Europe. This was the case in Spain in the years immediately before the establishment of its Inquisition. This prosperity, coupled with the fact that some Jews had considerable social independence and financial authority, was more fuel for the flames of anti-Semitism. Joseph Perez, a noted authority on the Spanish Inquisition, explained:

In medieval Spain, Jewish communities (known as aljamas) *... enjoyed relative autonomy ... They administered their own affairs, under the authority of their own magistrates. They had their own synagogues, schools, and cemeteries ... In this micro-society, as in [Spain's] dominant Christian society, the poor far*

outnumbered the rich. [But] a small minority of Jews practiced trade on a major scale and possessed fortunes which ... enabled them to lend money to kings [and other powerful] individuals. Sovereigns, [bishops] and great feudal lords were happy to leave ... the collection of taxes, tithes, and other dues [in Jewish hands]. It was this aspect of their activities that [particularly] fuelled ordinary people's hatred of the Jews.[24]*

Thus, average Christians in Spain associated Spanish Jews with taxes and monetary obligations. From there it was only a small step to believing that the poverty suffered by many Spanish Christians must also be the Jews' fault. It only took a little push, from a few angry people, to set anti-Semitic violence in motion. This eventually led to full-scale governmental persecution and a religious inquisition against the Jews. As Perez wrote:

Small groups of agitators had no difficulty in turning against the Jews the resentment of sections of the population driven to despair by a seemingly endless distress the causes of which they could not understand. They were shocked by the opulence [extreme wealth] of a minority of Jews and became convinced that they [the Christians] were the victims of an injustice.[25]

Anti-Jewish Violence Rises in Spain

In 1391 this distress by Spanish Christians finally boiled over. Urged on by Catholic clergymen, mobs in Seville, a major city in Castile, went on a rampage. They burned synagogues, looted Jewish homes, raped Jewish women, and killed Jewish leaders. The unrest quickly spread to Cordova and other Castilian towns. Then in August of that year, the anti-Jewish riots swept into Aragon, where Jews in Barcelona, Saragossa, Valencia, and other towns were targeted. Some 400 Jews were massacred in Barcelona and at least 250 died in Valencia.

Faced with this dangerous situation, some Jews fled the country. Most of these refugees settled in North Africa, France, or Portugal. Meanwhile many other Spanish Jews tried a different strategy to evade the persecution—converting to Christianity. Beginning in 1391, the year of the large and deadly anti-Jewish riots, the number of converted Jews, called conversos (Spanish for converted), increased each year for several decades. The exact figures for the number of conversions in this period are unknown, but scholars estimate that between 1391 and 1415, up to 200,000 Jews, half of all the Jews in Spain, were baptized.

Wanting to continue this trend, the Spanish authorities took steps designed to aid and strengthen it. In 1412 the advisors to the future King John II passed laws confining the Jews to ghettos (shabby, poor communities that were isolated from the rest of society). All Jewish men were also required to grow beards, and both male and female Jews had to sew red disks onto their outer garments to identify themselves as Jews. In addition, Jews were forbidden from becoming doctors, carpenters, blacksmiths, butchers, tailors, or tax collectors. Jews were also forced to listen to a minimum of three Christian sermons each year. At the same time, Dominicans and other Christian friars began preaching in the Jewish ghettos, trying to get more Jews to convert. These rules and practices were soon put into place in Aragon as well, and later in the century, King Ferdinand and Queen Isabella tightened the enforcement of anti-Jewish regulations. All of this was designed to make unconverted Jews so miserable that they would give in and become Christians.

The Growing Complaint Against False Christians

As the years went by, many Spanish Christians expressed some serious discontent with the conversos in the country. These feelings would eventually be expressed in the formation of the Spanish Inquisition during the reigns of King Ferdinand and Queen Isabella. Essentially, the growing complaint against the conversos was that they were false Christians. They were accused of leading a double life and trying to fool both the authorities and society. "It was said that in public

THE RISE OF QUEEN ISABELLA

Isabella, who created the Spanish Inquisition along with her husband, King Ferdinand, was born in Castile in 1451. She was the daughter of Castile's king, John II, and the half-sister of John's son, Henry, who ascended to the throne as Henry IV in 1454. In 1469, Isabella married Ferdinand, who at the time was the young heir to Aragon's throne. When King Henry IV died in December 1474, Isabella, then just 22, wasted no time in declaring herself queen of Castile. Some leading Castilians, as well as the king of Portugal, objected, but Ferdinand helped Isabella subdue all of her opponents. Not long afterward, the royal couple began implementing policies designed to bring the Spanish kingdoms together into a single, culturally unified nation. The creation of the Inquisition and the expulsion of the Jews were among these policies. In 1492, Isabella sponsored Christopher Columbus's first voyage across the Atlantic, which opened North and South America to Spanish explorers and initiated a global Spanish empire. Before she died in 1504, she had five children with Ferdinand, including Catherine of Aragon, who eventually married England's King Henry VIII.

they conformed with their obligations as Catholics," Perez explained, "going to mass, attending services, and distinguishing themselves as little as possible from other Christians." In the privacy of their homes, however, the conversos supposedly "observed the rites and practices of the law of Moses and respected the Jewish Sabbath and festivals."[26]

In 1475 some leaders of the Dominican order in Spain, along with various worried public officials, presented the charges against the conversos to Ferdinand and Isabella. At first these monarchs did not feel it was necessary to use violence against the converted Jews. Isabella, who had a prominent converso on her staff of advisors, was particularly reluctant to launch a persecution. However, Ferdinand was eventually convinced that force was the only viable option and he persuaded his wife to go along with him. The term Marrano (Spanish for pig) came to be used to refer to a Jew who had publicly converted but actually continued practicing Jewish traditions.

Their main goal in going after the conversos and Marranos, and later persecuting the remaining unconverted Jews in Spain, was to bring order and harmony to their country. Anti-Semitism, which had always existed in Spain, had intensified and was the cause of much public unrest. The two sovereigns reasoned that if the conversos were forced to become real and devout Christians, they would be accepted into Spanish society. At the same time, any Jews who refused to convert could be expelled from the country. The aim of these moves was to reduce the occurrences of anti-Semitism, which would restore public order. In turn, this would make Spain stronger and more united. In addition, Ferdinand had a lesser but still significant motive for going after the Jews: royal finances. An influential 19th-century Spanish writer named Juan Antonio Llorente wrote:

> The extirpation [eradication] of Judaism [in Spain] was not the real cause, but the mere pretext [excuse] for the establishment of the Inquisition by Ferdinand. The true motive was to carry on a vigorous system of confiscation against the Jews, and to bring their riches into the hands of the government.[27]

Formally Establishing the Spanish Inquisition

Whatever the combination of motives driving the Spanish monarchs to eliminate Judaism from Spain, they concluded that their efforts would be more effective if they had the authority and blessing of the Catholic Church. So in 1478, they contacted Pope Sixtus IV and asked him to approve their impending inquisition. Ferdinand and Isabella were pleased when, in November of that year, Sixtus issued a decree authorizing the establishment of the Spanish Inquisition.

In a strange move, the pope granted the right to appoint and dismiss the inquisitors to Ferdinand and Isabella. The normal procedure was for the Dominicans or local bishops to have these powers. The first inquisitors, Juan de San Martin and Miguel de Morillo, formally began operations in Seville in September 1480. They were soon joined by several advisors from the Spanish royal court. Ferdinand made it perfectly clear to the inquisitors what was expected of

Pope Sixtus IV, shown here, was unable to control the power he had given to Spain's rulers.

FORCIBLY BANISHING THE JEWS

After becoming grand inquisitor of the Spanish Inquisition in the early 1480s, Tomás de Torquemada repeatedly recommended to King Ferdinand and Queen Isabella that all unconverted Jews in Spain should be forcibly banished. De Torquemada argued that their continued presence would make it harder for the conversos to become devoted Christians, since they would still be seeing and hearing about their old traditions. Eventually, the monarchs agreed. On March 31, they issued the Alhambra Decree, or Edict of Expulsion: All Jews were given four months to leave the country. In one of the most shameful episodes in European history, over 100,000 Jews either went into exile or died in the process. Thousands were charged huge fees by ship captains and then thrown overboard in the open ocean. Thousands more were massacred and cut open by eager Christians who thought that Jews swallowed their jewelry to hide it. In addition, thousands of Jewish homes were looted or confiscated by Christians. Today, European Jews still remember the Spanish expulsion as a terrible act of cruelty and betrayal.

The Edict of Expulsion was seen as a triumph by the Spanish rulers but is seen as a tragedy by modern observers.

them and bluntly reminded them who was in charge, saying: "Although you and the others enjoy the title of inquisitor, it is I and the queen who have appointed you, and without our support you can do very little."[28] The inquisitors responded to these words by doing a great deal to please their masters. In the months that followed, hundreds of conversos were arrested and put on trial. Whether they were Marranos or truly converted, many of them received harsh sentences. The worst of these punishments was to be burned at the stake, which set an example for other suspected Marranos.

At first, there was a backlash against the inquisitors' methods and the harshness of the sentences they handed out. Some high-placed Spaniards, including many bishops, felt that it was inhumane—and un-Christian—to execute or otherwise punish conversos before at least giving them a chance to show that they could become devoted Christians. These critics complained to the pope, who expressed serious concerns about the way the new Inquisition was operating. On April 18, 1482, Pope Sixtus issued a statement making it clear that he felt the Spanish inquisitors were doing their jobs with too much intensity:

Many true and faithful Christians, on the testimony of [various sources] have without any legitimate proof been thrust into secular prisons, tortured, and condemned … deprived of their goods and property and handed over to the secular arm to be executed, to the peril of souls, setting a pernicious [bad] example, and causing disgust to many.[29]

King Ferdinand, as might be expected, was none too happy about the pope's statement. Feeling that he was trying to interfere with Spain's internal affairs, King Ferdinand wrote to him, saying:

Things have been told [to] me, Holy Father, which, if true, would seem to

Tomás de Torquemada, known as the Grand Inquisitor, has become a lasting symbol of the questionable practices of the Inquisition.

merit the greatest astonishment. It is said that Your Holiness has granted the conversos a general pardon for all the errors and offenses they have committed … To these rumors, however, we have given no credence … [You] have a duty to the Inquisition … Take care therefore not to let the matter go further … and entrust us with the care of this question.[30]

A stronger pope may well have told King Ferdinand that he was being impudent and continued to oppose the Spanish Inquisition. Sixtus was not a strong pope, and did not think that getting into a lengthy dispute with Ferdinand and Isabella was worth the time and effort. Soon after King Ferdinand's letter, he gave in and removed his former objections to the manner in which the new Inquisition was operating.

After Sixtus IV died in August 1484, his successor, Pope Innocent VIII, took the same weak stance. By this time, the Inquisition's leading figure, called the grand inquisitor, was a monk named Tomás de Torquemada, who over time became the historical model of a cruel and fanatical inquisitor. In order to make the Spanish sovereigns happy, Pope Innocent went so far as to grant de Torquemada the right to deal with all appeals lodged by those sentenced by the Inquisition. This was an enormous concession by the Church. In the earlier medieval Inquisition, appeals were handled by the archbishop of Seville. In this situation, de Torquemada, his inquisitors, and their royal patron, King Ferdinand, had the freedom to run the Inquisition virtually any way they desired. This was an ominous development. Without any substantial supervision from Rome, the way was open for the Inquisition in Spain to act in a terrible and cruel manner—which, as history shows us, it often did.

CHAPTER FOUR

PROCEDURES AND PENALTIES OF THE SPANISH INQUISITION

Much like the papal Inquisition that came before it, the Spanish Inquisition's goal was to end heresy. Also like the papal Inquisition, the Spanish Inquisition accomplished this by targeting, arresting, trying, and torturing suspects in an attempt to convert them to Christianity or kill them. At times, the tactics of the Spanish Inquisition varied. In addition, new rules and types of torture were also used. These differences separate the Spanish Inquisition from the tribunals that came before and after it, and make it distinct among other inquisitions.

The motivation of the Spanish Inquisition is another way it is different from the medieval Inquisition. During the earlier Inquisition, monarchs and popes were motivated mostly by religion. Most inquisitors during the medieval times believed they were saving the souls of the heretics they tried and punished. The papal Inquisition was seen by many as a crusade to protect and uphold the traditions and values of the Catholic Church. This was not the case with the Spanish Inquisition. Those who sought out heretics in Spain did not do it for religious reasons, but mostly for political purposes. Most inquisitors were not concerned with the souls of the heretics they tried, nor were they worried about protecting the Catholic Church. Instead, the Spanish Inquisition was driven by the political wishes of the king and queen. It was run by authorities separate from the Church whose main goal was to transform society. The Spanish Inquisition took place in an attempt to strengthen the country by way of

THE SPANISH INQUISITION EXPANDS

The Spanish Inquisition operated not only in Spain, but also in those lands that came under Spain's control in the late medieval and early modern eras. For example, between 1580 and 1640, the Spanish government controlled neighboring Portugal, and branches of the Inquisition opened in Lisbon and other Portuguese cities and towns. When this happened, many of the descendants of the Jews who had fled Spain and settled in Portugal in 1492 found themselves persecuted by inquisitors trying to force them to convert to Catholicism. The Spanish Inquisition also extended into the so-called New World, in colonies founded by the Spanish in North and South America. In addition to heretics, inquisitors in the Americas persecuted Spaniards and others who lived with or married Native Americans, who were viewed as inferior to Europeans.

purifying society and ridding it of unpleasant and unsafe heretics who were seen as a threat. As one inquisitor stated: "We must remember that the main purpose of the trial and execution [of an accused heretic] is not to save the soul of the accused, but to achieve the public good and put fear into others."[31]

The Spanish Inquisition was also organized differently than other European Inquisitions. During the papal Inquisition, all inquisitors were appointed by popes or bishops, who were also the final judges. In the Spanish Inquisition, it was the king who chose a grand inquisitor first, and only later received a blessing from the pope. In Spanish society, the grand inquisitor was a powerful figure who served as judge and mediator in all cases.

In addition to the grand inquisitor, the king also appointed a special council. It was known as El Consejo de la Suprema (The Supreme Council), and gave mandatory directives and advice to the inquisitor. The council, called the *Suprema* for short, eventually came to be one of the most feared and powerful groups in Spain. The more the Inquisition grew, the more powerful the Suprema became, and growing alongside it were the powers of the grand inquisitor himself.

Maintaining a State of Fear

These individuals were able to maintain a state of fear for more than three centuries because the procedures they employed were highly organized, extremely efficient, and frequently brutal and inhumane.

As in the earlier medieval Inquisition, the first step of their procedure involved targeting a specific town. The local inhabitants were ordered to attend a public meeting in which an inquisitor issued an Edict of Faith, which demanded that heretics confess their sins and that they and other citizens turn in suspected heretics. This almost always meant the accusation of people suspected to be Marranos. "The obligation to denounce all those whom one suspected of being heretics extended to all the faithful," Joseph Perez pointed out, "on pain of excommunication."[32] In this way, the threat of an ecclesiastical punishment—throwing someone out of the Church—was used to achieve a secular, political goal—to purge Jews, Muslims, Protestants, or other undesirables from society.

The Edict of Faith also supplied the potential informants in the town with the tools they needed to root out suspected heretics. For example, in the case of Spain's Marranos, the edict listed the various words and practices that were supposedly indications of a false Christian. One typical Edict of Faith issued in the 1500s in a number of Spanish towns went as follows:

If you know or have heard of anyone who keeps the Sabbath according to the law of Moses, putting on clean sheets and other new garments ...

on feast-days in honor of the Sabbath, and using no lights from Friday evening onwards; or if they have purified the meat they are to eat by bleeding it in water ... or have eaten meat in Lent and on other days forbidden by Holy Mother Church; or have fasted the great fast, going barefooted that day; or if they say Jewish prayers at night ... without making the sign of the cross ... or if they circumcise their children or give them Jewish names; or if after baptism they wash the place where the oil and chrism was put; or if anyone on his deathbed turns to the wall to die.[33]

One drawback of the process was that whether the suspects were Jews, Christians, or others, not all the denunciations made by citizens against their neighbors were related to religious faith. Frequently the informants targeted their social enemies or rivals or people who were just nonconformists. According to a 20th-century Spanish observer:

People could not bear to see anyone distinguishing himself, not thinking as others did, standing out from the herd. They could not tolerate ... personal opinions [or] thinking for oneself ... One had to stick to orthodoxy, the central dogma, the general opinion—or rather non-opinion [and] non-thought.[34]

This meant that the inquisitors had their work cut out for them in sifting through the many accusations of wrongdoing they received in the days and weeks following the Edict of Faith. Their initial job was to try to separate potential heretics from people who were Christian but had been denounced for being different than the norm. On occasion, when the inquisitors were unsure about how to proceed with an individual, they might ask for the advice of the Suprema. Eventually, the inquisitors built up files for various suspects. Each file contained evidence against these individuals in the form of testimony from neighbors and other local witnesses.

When the time seemed right, the inquisitors had the most likely suspects arrested and thrown in jail. Coinciding with the arrest, or *clamorosa*, the authorities seized some or all of the prisoners' property to help pay for their upkeep while confined. Wealthy suspects were allowed to bring one or two servants along with them into the Inquisition's prisons; these servants, who prepared food and performed other services, were stuck in the jail cells for as long as their masters remained in them. The prisoners were not allowed to write letters to or to communicate in other ways with outsiders. They they were forbidden to take Holy Communion or otherwise engage in regular worship (because they were assumed to be guilty of heresy against God).

The Process of Trying a Heretic

The length of time that an accused heretic spent in jail awaiting his or her trial varied widely. Sometimes it was only a few days or weeks; other times it was months or, in rare cases, more than a year. Eventually, when the grand inquisitor deemed that it was time for the trial to begin, he ordered armed guards to bring the accused person before a panel of judges. All of these judges were inquisitors who worked for the grand inquisitor. Yet another inquisitor acted as the prosecutor.

When the suspected heretic first faced the judges, one of them read aloud the charges against him or her. Then the judges proceeded to question the person. Among other things, they asked what he or she did for a living, the names of parents, grandparents, spouses, children and other relatives, the names of friends, and all the places where the person had lived or traveled to. The accused was also required to recite standard Catholic prayers and Bible facts to establish that he or she was or had been a Christian.

Next, the inquisitors tried to get the accused to confess to the crime of heresy. (That was generally the only charge; however, if the person

Trials in the Spanish Inquisition, such as this one, were overseen by many inquisitors.

was guilty of other crimes, he or she was expected to confess to those, too.) Unless the person confessed after the first time, the judges formally demanded a confession three times over a period of several days. The accused was presumed guilty unless he or she could prove otherwise. If the person refused to confess, the court appointed a lawyer to represent him or her. Unlike modern legal proceedings, however, the lawyer's job was not to defend the accused, but rather to persuade him or her to freely confess that they committed heresy. Finally, if the prisoner still refused to confess, the prosecutor brought in witnesses to prove that he or she was indeed guilty of the charges. During this phase of the trial, the accused was allowed to produce witnesses of his or her own, either to refute the prosecution's witnesses or to testify that the prisoner was an honest, moral person.

Rules for Torture: Rationalizing Brutality

The reason for the major emphasis on getting the accused to confess stemmed from the reality that, according to its own rules, the Inquisition could not convict or punish a person without a confession. The chief judge had to proclaim, *habemus confitentum reum* (we have a confessed criminal) before any sentence could be passed. The problem was that most of the people arrested by the Inquisition did not think of themselves as heretics, and a large portion of them were unwilling to admit to that charge. That meant that in many cases the inquisitors had to resort to some means to force the prisoners to confess. Because torture was already an accepted practice in the secular courts, it seemed only natural to use it in the inquisitional courts when forced confessions were required.

Over time, the Spanish Inquisition's various rules relating to the application of torture evolved. First, the inquisitors realized that torturing someone did not always make him or her tell the truth. As

Nicolas Eymerich, an inquisitor for the earlier medieval Inquisition, had written:

> *Torture itself is not a certain means of discovering the truth. There are weak men, who, at the slightest pain, confess even to crimes that they did not commit, and others, stronger and more stubborn, who will bear the greatest torments.*[35]

For this reason, it was not enough simply to accept the victim's confessions during torture. The accused was obliged to confirm his or her confession on the day following the torture, based on the notion that this time the admission was given freely, without coercion.

The trouble with this form of admission, which was nonetheless ignored by the inquisitors, is that the prisoner was likely confessing out of fear of being tortured again. According to the rules of the Spanish Inquisition, a person could be tortured only once during his or her trial. However, it was common knowledge that the inquisitors routinely got around this rule by calling the end of each torture session a "suspension." Thus, as Baigent and Leigh explained:

> *It could be claimed that a victim was indeed tortured only once, even if that "single" instance of torture included a multitude of*

CHRONICLES OF TORTURE DURING THE SPANISH INQUISITION

The courts of the Spanish Inquisition kept thorough and detailed records of nearly everything they did, including what happened in the torture sessions they held. Practically every word spoken (or paraphrases of them) in these sessions was written down by a clerk. Typical is this small portion of a session in which the inquisitors tortured a Belgian merchant because they did not believe his claims that he was a devout Catholic:

> They [the inquisitors] ordered him to be given three turns of the cord [on the rack] and when these were given he was warned [to confess], and he said he had nothing to say. Then they ordered another three turns of the cord, and he was warned and said that it was true he was a Catholic and had always been and that if it were otherwise, he would say so. He was admonished to tell the truth. He said he knew no more, and if he did he would say so. When he made this reply, they ordered another three turns of the cord, and when these were given, he was admonished [once again to tell the truth].[1]

1. Quoted in Walter de Gray Birch, *Catalogue of a Collection of Original Manuscripts of the Inquisition of the Canary Islands*. 2 vols. London, UK: Somerset, 1903, vol. 1, p. 378.

sessions and suspensions extended over a considerable period of time. And, of course, the victim was deprived of the hope that the end of any given session marked the end of his ordeal.[36]

Some of the other rules relating to the use of torture stipulated that it was inappropriate for the inquisitors themselves to shed blood. The local town executioner was often called to apply the torture instead of the inquisitors themselves. Typically these outside torturers were paid by the session. They often wore masks or hoods so that no one would recognize them, since the nature of their work made them extremely unpopular among the locals and potential targets for revenge.

Bloodless Methods of Torture

Because of the rule forbidding the shedding of blood during torture sessions, the inquisitors came to rely on certain methods that generally did not cause bleeding. Three such bloodless methods became very common in Spain. One, the *toca*, or water torture, involved forcing water down the victim's throat, forcing him or her to gag and creating the sensation of drowning. The person was tied to a board or ladder, which was tilted so that the victim's head was slightly lower than his or her feet. Sometimes a funnel was placed in the person's mouth and water poured into the funnel. Other times the torturer placed a cloth over the victim's mouth and kept wetting the cloth, which dripped water down the person's throat.

Also common was the *potro*, or rack torture. A rack was a large piece of wood with a wooden roller at each end. The torturers tied or chained the victim's arms and legs to the rollers and then forcefully turned the rollers, thereby stretching the victim until his or her joints throbbed with pain. There were variations of the *potro*, including some in which the ropes or chains pulled the limbs into unnatural positions. One such variation was described by William Lithgow, an English traveler captured by the Spanish in 1620 and subsequently tortured by the Inquisition. After surviving his ordeal and making it back to England, he wrote:

The executioner ... brought [me] to the rack and then mounted [me] on top of it ... The tormentor descended below, and drawing down my legs through the two sides of the three planked rack, he tied a cord about each of my ankles, and then ascending upon the rack, he drew the cords upward, and bending forward, with main [great] force my two knees against the two planks, the sinews of my two hams [hamstrings] burst asunder; and the lids of my knees [were] crushed.[37]

A third common torture employed by the Spanish Inquisition was the *garrucha* (called the *strappado* in Italy and some other parts of Europe), or pulley torture. The prisoner's feet were bound together and the hands were tied behind the back. The wrists were then attached to a rope that was itself connected to a pulley near the chamber's ceiling. Using this pulley system, the torturers raised the victim off the floor, causing severe pain to the wrists, arms, shoulders, and chest. One variation was to suddenly drop the prisoner to the floor, often resulting in dislocation of the ankles or knees.

In its later centuries, the Spanish Inquisition instituted other tortures even more gruesome than those just described. Whatever the nature of the torture implemented, it was not unusual for the victim to be permanently maimed or disabled. It was also possible for a suspect to die during torture. When this happened, the death was pronounced an unavoidable side effect of the torture;

This engraving shows a torture chamber during the Spanish Inquisition where multiple so-called heretics are tormented at once.

it was also seen as the victim's own fault, since if he or she had confessed in the first place, the inquisitors would not have been forced to apply torture.

Punishments for Those Who Survived

Those prisoners who survived the torture sessions (along with those who confessed beforehand to avoid torture) faced the verdict of the inquisitional court, followed by sentencing and punishment. Acquittals

PUBLIC DISPLAYS OF PUNISHMENT

The Spanish Inquisition regularly sponsored large-scale public ceremonies, known as autos-da-fé (acts of faith), in which people who had been convicted by the Inquisition were punished. This is part of a surviving contemporary description of an auto-da-fé held in February 1486 in the Spanish city of Toledo, in which the prisoners suffered public humiliation rather than death:

> All the [prisoners] went in procession, to the number of 750 persons, including both men and women ... The men were all together in a group, bareheaded and [barefoot] ... In their hands were unlit candles. The women were together in a group, their heads uncovered and their faces bare, unshod like the men and with candles ... With the bitter cold and the dishonor and disgrace they suffered from the great number of spectators ... they went along howling loudly and weeping and tearing out their hair ... At the door of the church were two chaplains who made the sign of the cross on each one's forehead ... Then they went into the church until they arrived at a scaffolding erected ... and on it were the father inquisitors ... [As punishment, the prisoners were ordered to whip themselves] ... and they were to fast for six Fridays. It was also ordered that all the days of their life they were to hold no public office ... [a]nd they were ordered that if they relapsed, that is if they fell into the same error again ... they would be condemned to the fire.[1]

1. Quoted in Henry Kamen, *The Spanish Inquisition*. London, UK: White Lion, 1976, pp. 190–191.

(being cleared of all charges) were very rare and generally happened only in cases in which it was proven that the witnesses who had accused the person had lied. Almost every person tried by the Inquisition throughout its long existence in Spain was found guilty and received some form of punishment.

These penalties varied widely, depending on the circumstances. Prisoners who confessed early on and were deemed to be sufficiently repentant received fairly light punishments. Among others, these included having to wear a large yellow sanbenito (a sleeveless coat) with a red cross on it to mark him or her as a sinner; having to recite lengthy prayers several times a day, sometimes for the rest of one's life; having to go on a religious pilgrimage to a holy Christian site and return with proof of the visit; and confiscation of part of the person's property.

Those prisoners who refused to

Autos-da-fé were common occurrences in Spain all throughout the Inquisition.

confess, as well as those who were arrested and tried by the Inquisition more than once, suffered progressively more severe punishments. These included public whippings, confiscation of all the person's property, prison sentences of various lengths, and death. In cases of the death penalty, the most common method was burning at the stake. This often took place at a large public ceremony known as an auto-da-fé in which hundreds or thousands of people gathered to watch burnings, whippings, and other punishments carried out by the Inquisition. The *autos* both demonstrated the great power wielded by the Inquisition in Spain and instilled fear in the populace. As Henry Kamen wrote, "We must take seriously the psychological impact of the atmosphere of an auto," and of the mere existence of the Inquisition as a pervasive institution in Spain. Many non-Catholics, Kamen pointed out, "were converted" to Catholicism "simply out of fear of being burnt alive."[38]

CHAPTER FIVE

THE NUMEROUS VICTIMS OF THE SPANISH INQUISITION

Monarchs in Spain during the 1400s created the Inquisition in an effort to unify their country. Kings and queens of the time period sought unification on religious, cultural, and political levels. More specifically, leaders in Spain wanted to be certain that the majority of the country was Catholic. Many conversos were accused of being Marranos or "false Christians." These were Jews who publicly converted to Christianity, but privately, and in secret, still worshiped as Jews. One goal of the Inquisition in Spain was to root out the Marranos. Between 1450 and 1500, as many as 2,000 Marranos were tried and executed.

In spite of the threats presented by the Inquisition, many Jews refused to convert to Christianity. To deal with those who refused to convert, in 1492 the Spanish monarchs issued a decree that called for all unconverted Jews to leave the country. This decree arose from King Ferdinand and Queen Isabella, who believed the majority of Jews would rather convert than leave their homes. This was a miscalculation. Many Jews chose exile instead of giving up their faith or worshipping in secret. Some who did convert practiced Judaism in private. What followed in Spain for a number of years was an inquisition focused on targeting, identifying, and eradicating secret Jews from Spanish society.

While Jews were the main targets of the Inquisition, Spanish leaders also focused their efforts on other non-Catholic groups who deviated from the traditional beliefs and practices of the church. Grand inquisitor de Torquemada targeted Muslims, as well as Protestants,

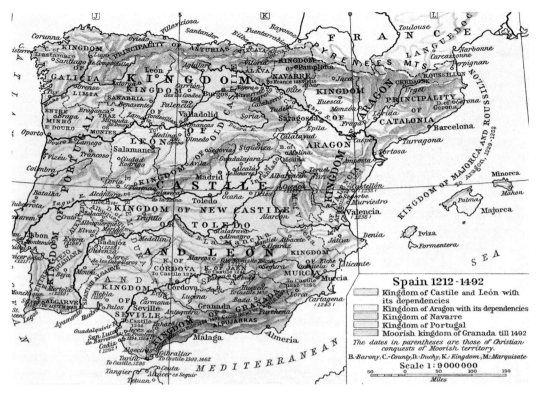

In this map of medieval Spain, the small Kingdom of Granada (in gray) is the only Muslim governmental authority on the overwhelmingly Catholic Iberian Peninsula.

and finally, Catholics whose ways of worship were considered unconventional. Longstanding prejudices against the Jews and Muslims of Spain were turned into inquisitional violence against those groups. Ferdinand and Isabella's plan to unite the country through religion was instead creating more divisions than ever among the people.

Singling Out the Muslims of Spain

Of the various non-Catholics targeted by the Inquisition, the next to be singled out after the conversos and Marranos were Spain's Muslims. In the earliest medieval centuries, Spain had been predominately Catholic. In the opening years of the 700s, armies of North African Muslims, often called Moors, swept into the Iberian Peninsula and seized most of its lands. Over the next several centuries, Muslims, Christians, and Jews coexisted in the region with a minimal amount of friction (excluding periodic persecutions of Jews, a common occurrence across Europe at the time).

Over time, however, Christian communities in Spain launched campaigns to regain control. In 1212, most

Muslims were driven from central Spain into Granada, a region that, at the time, covered much of the southern part of the peninsula. The last major refuge of Muslims in Spain, the kingdom of Granada persisted and for a while prospered, but in the centuries that followed, Castile and the other Christian kingdoms chipped away at it, steadily reducing its size. Finally, in 1492, King Ferdinand and Queen Isabella conquered Granada.

Because these Spanish monarchs dreamed of a Spain that was united both politically and culturally, the existence of large numbers of Muslims in the South presented a problem. Granada had long existed outside of

The Islamic forces of Granada are shown here surrendering to the victorious Christian Spanish.

Muslims are shown here submitting to Christian rule by being baptized into Catholicism.

the Spanish mainstream, so its inhabitants did not seem to pose much of a threat. At first the government's policy was to allow them to practice Islam as they pleased. In order to retain their religious freedom, Muslims were required to swear their loyalty to the Spanish crown. Those who did so were called Mudejares. This term derived from the Arabic word *mudajjan*, which means both "permitted to remain" and "tamed." The latter of these meanings shows the prejudice the Spanish had against Muslims. While it was assumed that most of them would end up converting to Christianity over time, there was still a considerable discrimination against them.

It did not take long for the more religiously conservative elements in Spain's government to grow impatient with this process, and in 1502 a new policy was announced. All Mudejares were ordered to convert to Christianity, and thereafter Spaniards who converted from Islam to Christianity were known as Moriscos (Spanish for little Moor). Just as with the Spanish

BAD BLOOD AND RACIAL PREJUDICE

The Spanish Inquisition not only questioned the religious views of its victims, but in some cases also employed its own version of racial bigotry. First, the Inquisition decided that both Jews and Muslims belonged to a different and inferior race from Catholic Spaniards. Then the inquisitors, backed by Spanish public officials, forbade those of "bad blood" from serving as public or religious officials. Moreover, all of the descendants of Jews and Muslims were discriminated against in the same manner for generations to come. Checking people's backgrounds and bloodlines to root out Jews continued in Spain until the mid-1800s. Even after the government abolished the practice in that century, anti-Jewish prejudice and fear of marrying someone with Jewish ancestry remained prevalent in Spanish society.

Jews, however, people questioned whether all of the Moriscos had truly converted. The common thought was that many Moriscos were retaining their old beliefs and rituals in private, and the government naturally turned to the Inquisition to deal with this problem. Just as they had learned to police and persecute Marranos, the inquisitors now began to watch for Moriscos who might be trying to fool society and the authorities.

Restraint in Dealing with Muslims

Looking back, it is noteworthy that for a number of years the Spanish Inquisition did not persecute Moriscos with the same intensity that it did Jewish conversos. The exact reasons for this policy are uncertain. It may have stemmed partly from the fact that Spanish Christians did not dislike Muslims in the same way they did Jews. Muslims were seen more as political and economic rivals who happened to have different beliefs, whereas Jews were viewed as the killers of Christ, degenerates who posed a direct threat to Christian faith. Also, it is possible that Ferdinand, Isabella, and their immediate successors felt that time would take care of the problem of the Moriscos. The leaders thought that living in an almost exclusively Catholic culture would cause Morisco children and grandchildren to grow up as Christians, and the old Islamic beliefs would steadily die out.

For these reasons and perhaps others, these monarchs ordered the inquisitors to show restraint in dealing with the Moriscos. This lenient policy is indeed reflected in the relatively low number of executions of Moriscos by the Inquisition in the 1500s. Between 1550 and 1600, only 27 Moriscos were found guilty of heresy by the Inquisition and burned at the stake. This did not last, however; in Valencia in the early 1600s, about 5,000 Moriscos died.

At the same time, however, rich Christian Spanish nobles saw the crackdown on the Moriscos as an opportunity to eliminate some economic competitors. Here again, the Inquisition could be a potent tool. As an instrument of the Spanish monarchy, the Inquisition could be used to reduce the political, social, and economic influence of the Moriscos, even if it did not imprison or execute large numbers of them. To facilitate this approach, they claimed that the Moriscos, like the Jews, supposedly belonged to a separate and inferior race from that of the local Christians. As Henry Kamen explained:

> Of the many burdens imposed on [the Moriscos] was the racialist cult of limpieza de sangre, or purity of blood, by which descendants of Muslims and Jews were forbidden to hold any public office, secular or ecclesiastical, in the kingdom ... In 1552 the Inquisition decided that no descendants of the two races could be appointed as familiars [secular servants working in churches and monasteries]. It had already been a rule that [conversos] were not allowed into the priesthood. In 1573 [this rule was] extended to cover Moriscos. Shut off this way from public office ... the Moriscos became relegated to the rank of second-class citizens, condemned to live permanently on the outer fringes of Spanish society.[39]

Eventually, even this amount of racial discrimination of Moriscos was not enough to satisfy the high-ranking Spanish who viewed them as a threat. (To make that threat seem even worse, some Spaniards spread the rumor that the Moriscos might help Moors from Africa invade and reconquer Spain, a charge that was not credible.) Several proposed plans to deal with the Moriscos circulated in the late 1500s. They included purging them by unleashing the Inquisition's full resources against them, castrating all males so that the race would soon die out, and shipping them all to Newfoundland, where they would likely die from the cold and other harsh conditions.

These plans were rejected in large part simply on logistical grounds. By 1600, there were at least 300,000 Moriscos in Spain. The Inquisition possessed considerable, but still limited, resources and its leaders realized that arresting, imprisoning, trying, and punishing such enormous numbers of people would be far too expensive and difficult. It would also

FINDING SECRET MUSLIMS

When the Spanish Inquisition entered a town and delivered an Edict of Faith, it generally alerted the townspeople to certain signs by which to identify heretics. Regarding Moriscos (converted Muslims) who might still be practicing Islam in secret, scholar Joseph Perez summarized the signs an edict gave to identify them:

> The edict cited the customs of celebrating particular days and particular festivals, of fasting during Ramadan [a Muslim holiday], of slaughtering animals in a particular way, of performing ritual ablutions (washing arms, hands, the face, the mouth, the nose, ears, legs, and private parts), and abstaining from the consumption of wine and pork ... washing the dead, enveloping them in a clean shroud, burying them lying on their side, [and] placing a stone close to the head, along with honey, milk and other food for the soul of the deceased.[1]

1. Joseph Perez, The Spanish Inquisition. Trans. Janet Lloyd. New Haven, CT: Yale University Press, 2005, p. 138.

be impossible for either the government or the Inquisition to perform mass castrations or relocations. Finally the government and leaders of the Inquisition decided that, just as they did with Jews, the best course was simply to force all Moriscos to leave the country. In 1609, King Philip III issued an expulsion decree similar to the one that had targeted the Jews in 1492. Nearly all of the Moriscos left in the five years that followed. (Some went to North Africa; there, ironically, they met with prejudice because they were seen as Christians. Others ended up in France and Tunisia.)

The Protestant Threat Increases

Part of the reason that the leading inquisitors were reluctant to go after the Moriscos on a massive scale in the late 1500s and early 1600s was because by that time the Inquisition had its hands full trying to deal with a wide variety of perceived heretics. Until about 1524, the Spanish Inquisition had been mainly concerned with persecuting Jews and Muslims. In that year the inquisitors first realized that a potentially much larger threat loomed on the horizon—Protestantism.

The Protestants emerged in Europe rather suddenly. For roughly 900 years there had been only one

Martin Luther was the founder of the first Protestant religion, which was later called Lutheranism.

Christian authority in Europe—the Roman Catholic Church. However, in the late 1400s and early 1500s the Church's leadership came under increasing criticism from within. Believing that the organization had become rich and materialistic and strayed too far from basic Christian principles, some earnest clergymen demanded major reforms.

The situation reached its breaking point in 1517. An outspoken German professor of theology named Martin Luther publicly issued a list of charges against the Church. He criticized the excess wealth and luxury enjoyed by the pope, the bishops, and the large bureaucracy of religious officials surrounding them. Luther wanted the pope and bishops to return to the simplicity and honesty supposedly displayed by the earliest Christian leaders and to better address the spiritual and earthly needs of ordinary members of their flocks. He argued that the clergy's accumulation of extreme wealth was directly against Christian teachings.

The pope warned Luther to cease these protests. When he refused, he was excommunicated. In response, the brash Luther and his fast-growing army of supporters broke free of the Church and established a new branch of Christianity, which became known as Lutheranism. By the mid-1520s, Lutheranism, the first Protestant group, was well established in many parts of Europe and other Protestant groups were in the midst of forming. At least at first, basic Protestant beliefs were not significantly different than traditional Catholic ones. What initially differentiated the Protestants was their refusal to acknowledge the central authority of the pope. Moreover, they began a series of reforms to attempt to correct the abuses that Luther had protested.

The Growing Lutheran Threat

For the most part, the Catholic Church could do little about the Lutherans and other Protestants. The pope could not send his own papal inquisitors to silence and punish Protestants because there were simply too many of these dissenters, and they were spread all across Europe. The situation was different within Spain, however. The country only had about 7 or 8 million people in total, the vast majority of whom were still firmly devoted to the Catholic Church. The Spanish Inquisition was already well established and quite experienced at rooting out and dealing with heretics and nonconformists. For the Spanish monarchs and their inquisitors, therefore, the goal became to keep Protestantism from gaining a strong foothold in the country.

To accomplish that goal, the minions of the Inquisition sought to keep the bulk of the Spanish population insulated from outside Protestant influences. Initially, they worried mainly about Lutheran influences, since the Lutherans were the first and one of the most vocal of the emerging Protestant branches. One source of contamination was Lutheran books and pamphlets being smuggled into Spain. It came to the attention of the inquisitors that Spanish conversos now living in the Netherlands were translating Lutheran writings into Spanish and secretly shipping them into Spain. In 1524, the Inquisition arrested a German merchant who had brought some Lutheran literature to Valencia. In that same year, a foreign merchant ship was caught with two barrels filled with Lutheran books; agents of the Inquisition and local authorities promptly burned the volumes on the nearest beach and arrested the ship's captain. So paranoid were the inquisitors about the threat of Lutheran ideas that even a monk who had bought a Lutheran book and burned it was arrested because he had looked through it before destroying it.

The inquisitors considered an actual conversion from Catholicism to Lutheranism to be an even greater crime. At first it was mainly foreign merchants and other outsiders who were arrested for being Lutherans. Joseph Perez described one celebrated incident that occurred in San Sebastian in 1539:

> [Several] English traders and sailors were denounced to the ... Inquisition for making suspect [remarks] in the course of a brawl in the harbor. A Spaniard had apparently said that all English were Lutherans and the English had retorted that their country's religion was better than that practiced in Spain. You did not have to fast in order to win salvation, nor did you have to confess your sins to any man ... but only to God. Six of these Englishmen were put on

trial for Lutheranism; some were sentenced to pay small fines or to recant publicly. Only one received a prison sentence. He managed to escape, was recaptured ... [and] was burned at the stake.[40]

As time went on, however, some Spaniards were arrested for choosing Lutheranism. In 1542 the Inquisition arrested, convicted, and executed a Spanish businessman named Francisco de San Roman, who had converted to Lutheranism after he had been exposed to that faith on a trip to Belgium. Another Spaniard who became a Lutheran, Miguel Servet, actually published a book in which he rejected many Catholic ideas. Servet was smart enough to leave the country before the agents of the Inquisition could find and arrest him. In an ironic twist, however, he also angered members of another emerging Protestant sect, Calvinism, and in 1553 some Calvinists burned him at the stake in Geneva, Switzerland.

The biggest concentrations of Lutherans in Spain were discovered in 1558 in two of Spain's largest cities, Valladolid and Seville. Among those arrested were monks, nuns, and several nobles. The number of accused Lutherans was so high that the local prisons could not hold them all, and there were not enough local inquisitors to conduct all the trials,

Although Miguel Servet escaped capture from the Spanish Inquisition, he was later convicted of heresy by Calvinists in Geneva, Switzerland, and burned at the stake.

so extra inquisitors were brought in from other cities. In large autos-da-fé held in 1559 and 1560, more than fifty people were burned at the stake for embracing Lutheranism. Hundreds more received prison sentences. It is noteworthy that these persecutions horrified Lutherans and other Protestants in other parts of Europe, and they inspired the first of many Protestant denunciations of the Spanish

WITCHES AS AN INQUISITIONAL TARGET

The Spanish Inquisition did prosecute a number of people for witchcraft, but in its first three centuries of existence, only a relative handful were executed for it, especially when compared to the hundreds of thousands of supposed witches burned to death in other parts of Europe in this period. In most cases, the Spanish inquisitors took the stance that witchcraft was difficult to prove and was probably only a superstition. In 1611, Alonso de Salazar, a special deputy of the Suprema, interviewed or studied the confessions of nearly 2,000 confessed witches, both male and female, and later concluded:

> With all the Christian attention in my power, I have not found even indications from which to infer that a single act of witchcraft has really occurred ... Moreover, my experience leads to the conviction that, of those availing themselves of the Edict of Grace, three-quarters and more have accused themselves and their accomplices falsely ... I deduce ... that there were neither witches nor bewitched until they were talked and written about. This impressed me recently [in a town] where those who confessed stated that the matter started there [only] after [a clergyman] came there to preach about these things.[1]

1. Quoted in Henry C. Lea, *A History of the Inquisition of the Middle Ages*. 4 vols. New York, NY: Harbor Press, 1955, vol. 4, pp. 233–234.

Inquisition that would occur over the course of more than three centuries. (It is worth noting the degree of anti-Semitism all across Europe: no objections to the Spanish Inquisition were made when they executed and exiled thousands of Jews.)

Going After Other Religious Groups

The inquisitors in Spain did not limit their targets to just Jews, Muslims, and Protestants. Other groups whose members seemed to deviate from Catholic ideas and rituals in the slightest ways became suspects of the Inquisition as well. Among these other groups were women known as the beatas (Spanish for pious women). Most of them were unmarried women who felt some connection to God and decided to devote their lives to him. Though not nuns in the strict sense, the beatas did resemble nuns, as they lived in secluded, monastery-like homes and spent most of their time in prayer and other spiritual activities. Often people from nearby communities would visit the beatas, who would give advice or provide spiritual comfort.

The Inquisition did not begin persecuting beatas until the second half of the 16th century, and it arrested and charged only a small percentage of them. The precise reasons that the inquisitors persecuted some of the beatas and not others are somewhat unclear. It is likely that those who were arrested were suspected of practicing some sort of magic. It is also possible the inquisitors may have found it offensive that these women claimed to have a special relationship with God, even though they were not formal members of the Catholic clergy. The total number of beatas convicted by the Inquisition is unknown.

In addition to entire groups of people, the Inquisition opposed and persecuted numerous individuals who were viewed as dangerous. Even prominent members of the Catholic clergy were not immune. Such was the case of Bartholome Carranza, Archbishop of Toledo, who was one of Spain's leading Catholics. In 1559 he was arrested on two charges. First, Carranza was accused of using terminology from the Lutheran religion while preaching; second, the archbishop had written a religious pamphlet that contained ideas the inquisitors felt did not follow official Catholic beliefs accurately. Because of the high rank he held within the Church, Carranza was able to appeal to Pope Pius to intervene. Pius did so. In a strange turn of events, he agreed to Carranza's requests to see him in Rome. The Spanish government reluctantly gave in and the archbishop was eventually released in Italy. Carranza was one of the few people arrested by the Spanish Inquisition who managed to escape its wrath.

CHAPTER SIX

THE NEW INQUISITION AND THE THREAT OF MODERN SCIENCE

While the Spanish Inquisition was preoccupied with suppressing Jews and Muslims, Protestantism was on the rise, both across Europe and within Spain's borders. Starting in the early 1500s, numerous groups were finding flaws with the central Catholic Church and forming their own religious branches. Though the inquisition in Spain attempted to nip these growing sects in the bud, the rest of Catholic Europe was unable to stop the increasing tide of unhappy Christians. The work done by these Protestant groups to restore the people's faith is now called the Reformation. Even though most Protestant leaders were only interested in preaching the word of God to as many people as possible, the pope and other Church leaders were worried that their control over Europeans would decline as people started to follow these new religions.

Unfortunately for the Catholic leaders, the Reformation was not the only growing threat to their absolute power. For centuries, the Church had been able to control the flow of information to the people. This allowed them to censor any dangerous topics, books, and thinkers before they could reach the masses. However, as technology and literature continued to advance, assisted by the invention of the printing press in 1440, Europeans grew more and more knowledgeable—especially about science.

While today this might be a positive turn of events, it was a major negative for the Church as it began to feel its power slipping. "Knowledge, so the cliché goes, is power," Baigent and Leigh pointed out, *and the Church wielded power largely through the knowledge it monopolized, commanded, controlled, and made available to the lay populace [common people] only [very carefully]. With the Reformation, this situation changed dramatically. The Reformation witnessed a veritable explosion of knowledge. It was to issue from secular sources. It was to issue from the newly established Protestant "heresies," such as Lutheranism ... Luther's translation of the Bible into the vernacular [common language] and other translations that followed ... [made] scripture available for the first time to the layman [average person], who could read it for himself without the ... filtering apparatus of the priesthood.*[41]

As it had always done, the Church immediately started making moves to protect its position of power. Catholic leaders wanted to stop the conversion of followers to the Protestant religions while also slowing down the rapid flow of knowledge to the commoners. With Pope Paul III at the helm, there was a major reorganization of the Church, beginning in the 1540s. In order to reinforce Catholic ideals and help destroy heretics, they created a new inquisition, officially titled the Congregation of the Holy Roman and Universal Inquisition, or Holy Office. Today it is often referred to as the Roman Inquisition, but at the time it was simply called the Holy Office.

Partially following in the footsteps of the Spanish Inquisition, this new tribunal created the position of an inquisitor-general, who would oversee the lower inquisitors. The first man in this powerful office was Cardinal Giovanni Carafa. He demonstrated a ruthless desire to punish any and all heretics and threats to the Church—and to do so severely.

Pope Paul III initiated a new and powerful version of religious tribunal, now called the Roman Inquisition.

The Roman Inquisition's First Victims

Indeed Caraffa was ready to institute nothing less than a reign of terror, believing that the Church was desperate, and therefore needed to take desperate measures. Paul III and his successor, Julius III, were not as zealous as Carafa, and kept him from abusing the great powers of the inquisitional office. However, in 1555, Carafa himself ascended to the Church's throne as Pope Paul IV. From that moment until it was disbanded, the Roman Inquisition became a force to be reckoned with in Europe.

One of the first major orders from the new pope was to censor books and other writings. This was done as a way of controlling the distribution of ideas that might damage the Church's image and credibility. In 1559, the pope and Inquisition issued the *Index Librorum Prohibitorum* (list of banned books), often called the papal index. Near the top of the list, not surprisingly, were Martin Luther's writings, as well as the books and pamphlets of other Protestant authors. In addition, Jewish holy writings, including the Talmud, were banned, as well as the new, non-Latin translations of the Bible.

In addition to banning books, the newly empowered Roman Inquisition went after some of the same

Cardinal Carafa (later Pope Paul IV) used an iron fist when dealing with those he considered heretics.

groups that had been targeted by the medieval and Spanish Inquisitions. In 1556, for example, 24 converted Jews suspected of retaining their traditional rituals were arrested, tried, and burned in Ancona (a town situated northeast of Rome). Reviving a feud that was hundreds of years old, the Inquisition also went after Waldensians wherever it could find them.

Persecuting what the Church considered traditional groups of heretics occupied relatively little of the Roman Inquisition's time and energy, however. More often than not, the Holy Office concentrated on going after prominent individuals. They targeted writers, philosophers, scientists, and would-be religious reformers—anyone whose ideas and public voices might be major threats to the Catholic Church. By making examples of these high-profile heretics, inquisitors tried to discourage others from committing heresy. Even members of the Catholic hierarchy were not immune from prosecution. In 1557, for instance, the Inquisition arrested and imprisoned a cardinal (a rank in the Church second only to that of the pope). Other prominent individuals that were silenced by the Roman Inquisition include an Italian scholar beheaded in 1567 and an Italian university professor strangled to death three years later. In 1573, the Venetian painter Paolo Veronese was charged with heresy for including a dog and a servant with a bloody nose in a scene depicting the Last Supper of Christ. The artist escaped serious punishment by changing the setting and name of the painting to a *Feast in the House of Levi.*

The Holy Office also tried to silence a noted Italian philosopher and writer named Tomasso Campanella. Campanella was an interesting historical figure. He spent 27 years in prison for plotting to overthrow the Spanish crown, and during this time he wrote a book called *The City of the Sun.* This drew the attention of the Inquisition in several ways. First, he claimed that experience is as important as religious faith in the study of philosophy. He also questioned certain philosophical and scientific principles accepted by the Church. Shortly after he was released by Spain, he was arrested again, this time in Rome, for his heretical writing. He was able to negotiate his way out of prison after three years.

Tomasso Campanella was one of the many intellectuals who were targeted by the Inquisition.

THE WORLD IS NOT FLAT

The Roman Inquisition tried to maintain conformity of belief in the worldview the Catholic Church embraced at that time. Largely, that view followed the ideas of the ancient Greek scholar Aristotle. In his treatise *On the Heavens*, Aristotle offered the following evidence to prove that Earth is a sphere:

> As it is, the shapes which the Moon itself each month shows are of every kind—straight, gibbous, and concave—but in eclipses the outline is always curved; and since it is the interposition of the Earth [between the Sun and Moon] that makes the eclipse, the form of this line will be caused by the form of the Earth's surface, which is therefore spherical.[1]

1. Quoted in Morris R. Cohen and I. E. Drabkin, *A Source Book in Greek Science*. Cambridge, MA: Harvard University Press, 1948, p. 148.

Science Challenges the Church

Although Campanella was not a scientist by trade, some of his ideas dealt with scientific principles and questioned some of the accepted scientific concepts of the day. (While in jail, Campanella went so far as to write a statement of support for the famous astronomer Galileo Galilei while he battled with the Inquisition.) Indeed, in the eyes of the Church and the Inquisition, the onrush of modern science was even more threatening than the appearance of new philosophical and religious ideas.

One reason that new scientific ideas suddenly seemed so threatening was simply that, for most of the Middle Ages, there had been little scientific progress. Fully supported by the Church, standard views of nature and the universe had conformed to those of ancient Greek scholars, especially the fourth–century BC philosopher and mathematician Aristotle. He had theorized that Earth is a large sphere that rests at the center of the universe. (As proof, he cited the fact that falling objects everywhere always move toward the center of Earth; he was unaware that gravity is the real cause.) Aristotle also taught that the universe consisted of a series of large, invisible spheres that nested within one another. He argued that every planet, moon, or star moved along the surface of each sphere. From the 1300s to the 1500s, the Catholic Church agreed with these ideas and incorporated them into its own scientific worldview. The most important aspect of this view was that Earth and humanity together were the centerpiece of God's creation.

However, some late medieval scholars came to the conclusion that this Earth-centered, or geocentric, view of the universe was in error. The great turning point came in 1543, when Polish astronomer Nicolaus Copernicus proposed a sun-centered, or heliocentric, view. According to Copernicus in his *On the Revolutions of the Heavenly Spheres*:

> The sun is the center of the universe. Moreover, since the sun remains stationary, whatever appears as a motion of the sun is really due rather to the motion of the Earth ... The size of the universe is so great that the distance Earth-sun is imperceptible in relation to the sphere of the fixed stars. This should be admitted, I believe, in preference to perplexing the mind with an almost infinite multitude of spheres, as must be done by those who kept the Earth in the middle of the universe.[42]

The Church viewed these statements as both a clear challenge and a substantial threat. Copernicus's book ended up on the Holy Office's list of forbidden writings almost immediately.

Targeting Giordano Bruno

Despite the fact that the Church frowned on Copernicus's theory, his ideas steadily gained followers in some scholarly circles. Among the leading Copernicans of the 16th century was Giordano Bruno, an Italian monk who became a poet, philosopher, and brilliant astronomer. An outspoken, argumentative, and fearless individual, Bruno did more than accept and support the idea that Earth is a part of the sun's planetary system. He also argued that there must be planetary systems orbiting other stars; moreover, he said, there are surely intelligent beings inhabiting the planets in those systems. In 1585, in a work titled *The Ash Wednesday Supper*, he stated:

> Our world, called the terrestrial globe, is identical as far as material composition goes with the other worlds, the [orbiting] bodies of other stars; and ... it is childish to ... believe otherwise. Also ... there live and strive on them [the distant planets] many and innumerable ... individuals to no less extent than we see these living and growing on the back of this [Earth] ... Once this is admitted, many secrets of nature, hitherto hidden, do unfold.[43]

Such ideas were bound to attract the attention of the Inquisition. So Bruno eventually left Italy, where the reach of the inquisitors was strongest, and began lecturing and preaching in various foreign countries, including Germany, France, and England. He taught for a while in France. There he also enjoyed the protection of a

After his refusal to recant Copernicus's sun-centered universe theory, Giordano Bruno was tried and eventually executed.

a noble friend in 1591, however, he took a chance and returned to his native country. After that noble friend was unhappy with Bruno's desire to leave Italy and return to Germany, he denounced the philosopher to the Holy Office, which ordered his arrest. Bruno was tried for heresy in Venice, but the trial was actually looking to be in his favor. It did not take long for the Roman Inquisition in Rome to demand he stand trial before them, instead.

When he refused to take back his beliefs about the universe, the inquisitors began torturing him. For the seven years of his trial he repeatedly suffered unbelievably cruel physical abuse, but his tormentors were never able to break him. Through it all, he remained steadfast; he was even bold enough to try to convert the inquisitors to Copernicus's theory. Finally, the leaders of the Holy Office decided that they had had enough of Bruno. At their order, on February 17, 1600, he was burned at the stake in Rome. They also ordered that the scientist be gagged while on his way to the scaffold, to keep him from contaminating the spectators with his heresies.

number of noblemen, including King Henry III, who shielded him from the Roman Inquisition's henchmen. During his travels, Bruno wrote around 20 books, advocating, among other things, that the universe is infinite in scope.

As long as Bruno stayed out of Italy and remained surrounded by people who respected his work, the agents of the Inquisition were unable to arrest him. After being invited to Venice by

The Brilliant Galileo Galilei

Bruno's persecution and execution demonstrated that it was not

THE CHURCH ACKNOWLEDGES
ITS MISTAKES

In 1992, Pope John Paul II became the first Catholic leader to publicly admit that the Church and its inquisitors had been wrong in arresting and punishing Galileo in the 1600s. Among other things, John Paul said:

> The problem posed by theologians of that age was ... the compatibility between heliocentrism and Scripture. Thus the new science, with its methods and the freedom of research which they implied, obliged theologians to examine their own criteria of scriptural interpretation. Most of them did not know how to do so. Paradoxically, Galileo, a sincere believer, showed himself to be more perceptive in this regard than the theologians who opposed him ... The majority of theologians did not recognize the formal distinction between Sacred Scripture and its interpretation, and this led them unduly to transpose into the realm of the doctrine of the faith a question which in fact pertained to scientific investigation ... In fact, the Bible does not concern itself with the details of the physical world, the understanding of which is the competence of human experience and reasoning.[1]

1. Quoted in *L'Osservatore Romano*, November 4, 1992, pp. 3–4.

yet safe to agree with Copernicus's views openly, but that did not keep many perceptive scientists and other intellectuals from concluding that these views were right. Sooner or later, some prominent individual was bound to challenge the Church again on these matters and in so doing become a martyr to the cause of modern science.

That martyr, and by far the most famous opponent of the Church and Inquisition in this period, turned out to be a younger contemporary of Bruno's: the brilliant Italian scientist Galileo Galilei. Born in the northern Italian town of Pisa on February 15, 1564, Galileo became an early supporter of Copernicus's heliocentric theory, but the young scientist was more cautious than Bruno and kept his support private. For fear of the Inquisition's wrath, Galileo long refrained from publicly endorsing the Copernican theory. Part of the reason for this strategy was that he felt there was not yet enough powerful evidence to convince the religious authorities that the heliocentric view was correct.

Galileo eventually came to believe that he had the evidence he needed to change the minds of Church leaders, which would have been a great leap forward for science. In 1609 he heard that some Dutch glassmakers had recently invented a device that used a system of lenses to magnify images of distant objects. It became known as the telescope. Galileo soon built his own telescope and became the first person ever to use such an instrument to study what we now call outer space. In November 1609, he gazed through his telescope at the moon and saw that its surface is covered with craters and mountain chains. A few months later Galileo discovered the four largest moons of Jupiter. He deduced that their movements around that planet were definitive proof that not all objects in space revolve around Earth. This meant that the geocentric view of the universe was false. Surely, he thought, the leaders of the Church would believe the evidence of their own eyes.

However, Galileo was wrong. Many Church officials simply refused to look through the scientist's telescope, while others flatly informed him that Copernicus's ideas had to be wrong, regardless of what they saw. In addition, a prominent Dominican friar, Tommaso Caccini, called science in general the work of the devil and to believe that the earth moves around the sun was heresy.

Earnestly but foolishly, Galileo, who was a devout Catholic, felt he had a duty to guide the Church away from their outdated views and toward reasonable scientific principles. So he spent several years writing a book that discussed in detail the leading astronomical opinions of the day, including the heliocentric view. The book, titled *Dialogue Concerning the Two Chief World Systems—Ptolemaic and Copernican*, was completed in 1630. The official Catholic censor in Rome reviewed and approved it. When

Galileo constructed a telescope and found evidence that the earth rotated around the sun. This proof gave Galileo hope that Church leaders would be convinced that Copernicus's theories were correct.

it appeared in print in February 1632, it was quickly sold out to a populace hungry for knowledge. These developments convinced Galileo that the Church was ready to embrace modern scientific ideas.

The Trial of Galileo

However, once again the scientist had miscalculated. Only a few months after the book's publication, the Church reversed itself and halted any further printings. The pope turned the matter over to the Roman Inquisition, which ordered Galileo to stand trial for heresy. In April 1633 he was confined to the building in Rome that housed the offices of the Inquisition.

Because he had long been friendly with the pope and a number of cardinals and bishops, he was not thrown into a dungeon; he instead occupied a comfortable suite of rooms and was allowed a servant to help him with his daily needs.

The trial consisted of four interrogation sessions, called depositions, in which a panel of inquisitors questioned Galileo with the intention of establishing his heresy. During these sessions, he was allowed to make statements in his own defense. Later,

SPECIAL TREATMENT FOR GALILEO

Unlike many other victims of the Roman Inquisition, Galileo was not physically abused, isolated, or abandoned during his imprisonment. In fact, he lived in a comfortable apartment and enjoyed the support of a number of high-placed churchmen, including some of the inquisitors. These supporters agreed that the scientist was guilty of advocating Copernicus's heliocentric theory, but they also agreed that Galileo was a good man who did not deserve to be humiliated. One friendly churchman, Father Vincent Firenzuola, met privately with Galileo and assured him that if he admitted he had erred, it could be arranged for him to receive a light sentence—perhaps only a few months of house arrest. Firenzuola later recalled:

> I entered into discourse with Galileo ... and after many arguments ... had passed between us, by God's grace, I ... brought him to a full sense of his error, so that he clearly recognized that he had ... gone too far in his book ... He requested, however, a little time in order to consider the form in which he might most fittingly make the confession.[1]

1. Quoted in Giorgio de Santillana, *The Crime of Galileo*, Chicago, IL: The University of Chicago Press, 1955, p. 252.

Galileo stood trial before the Holy Office on the charge of heresy for claiming that the sun is the center of the universe.

the inquisitors reported the outcomes of the depositions to ten cardinals who had been selected to be Galileo's judges. Because he refused to take back his claims, the forthcoming guilty verdict was inevitable. In what constituted the second part of the trial, they debated what sentence to give the scientist and imposed that sentence.

The Inquisition did find Galileo guilty of heresy. Part of the official sentence handed down by the judges read as follows:

We ... declare that you, Galileo ... have rendered yourself ... vehemently [very strongly] suspected of heresy, namely, of having believed and held the doctrine—is false and contrary to the sacred and divine Scriptures—that the Sun is the cen-

ter of the world and does not move ... First, with a sincere heart and unfeigned faith, you [must] abjure [renounce], curse, and detest before us the aforesaid errors and heresies ... In order that this your grave and pernicious error ... may not remain altogether unpunished ... we condemn you to the formal prison of this Holy Office during our pleasure.[44]

Following these orders, on June 22, 1633, Galileo, then 69 years old, knelt before leading members of the Church and Inquisition and declared that he did not believe that Earth moved around the sun. "I must altogether abandon the false opinion that the sun is the center of the world and immovable,"[45] he stated. By doing this he was spared the death sentence, but compromised his scientific ideals. Thereafter, the defeated scientist remained under house arrest until his death in January 1642.

There is no doubt that the leaders of the Roman Inquisition felt they had triumphed by forcing Galileo to recant. They believed that they had made an example of him and this would prevent new ideas from challenging traditional, cherished Church doctrines. However, this attitude was little more than self-delusion. The reality was that modern science, far from being defeated, was just beginning to gain acceptance. Moreover, though no one could foresee it at the time, the Inquisition's own days as a powerful institution were almost over.

THE INQUISITION AND ITS LEGACY

Even after the Inquisition ended, the Church still retained a strong opinion against modern science and technology. For example, in the centuries that followed the trial of Galileo, the Church remained firm on its stance against the heliocentric theory. It was only after both the Church and the Inquisition began to lose power that the outdated geocentric theory was eventually discarded.

As late as 1819, the writings of both Copernicus and Galileo were banned by the papal index. In addition, the Church's own astronomers avoided publishing theories or speaking publicly on the heliocentric theory. This was all in spite of the fact that by the 1700s, heliocentric theory was a commonly accepted fact in most scientific communities worldwide.

In 1822, Pope Pius VII was persuaded to send the matter regarding the sun-centered universe to the Holy Office, so that the Holy Office might consider changing its opinion on the subject.

In fact, it was not until astronomer Canon Settele asked Pope Pius VII if the Church might consider modernizing its stance on heliocentric theory. In response, Pius turned the matter over to the Holy Office. Finally, in 1822, the Church reversed its opinion, issuing the following statement in September of that year. "The printing and publication of works treating of the motion of the Earth and the stability of the sun, in accordance with the opinion of modern astronomers, is permitted at Rome."[46]

The End of the Inquisition

The tolerance of this statement, relative to the highly conservative views of the Inquisition, is immediately striking. What happened to that once-stern and greatly feared institution to make it sound so open-minded and reasonable? The answer is that no single event caused the Inquisition to change. Rather, a long series of political, religious, and scientific events and trends made the older, more forceful Inquisition outdated. Over time, Church leaders had altered its mission and methods accordingly.

One of the major factors in the decline of the old Inquisition was the sudden rise of enlightened political thinking and democratic revolutions in Europe. First came the European Enlightenment, which began in the late 1600s and lasted until the early 1800s. This intellectual movement was driven primarily by liberal English, French, and eventually American thinkers. It celebrated human reason, scientific facts, religious toleration, the existence of certain basic natural human rights, and fair government. Enlightenment philosophers argued that science might reveal the true nature of the world, which humans could then remake, control, and exploit to their advantage. The Enlightenment's ideas steadily and significantly changed the way educated people, especially Europeans, viewed the political and social institutions that had been taken for granted over hundreds of years. Among these institutions were the Catholic Church and the Inquisition, both of which had been seen by Protestants and other non-Catholics as old-fashioned and in need of reform for years. Even some devout Catholics began to agree with this position.

These feelings about the Inquisition were expressed in dramatic fashion during the late 1700s. In 1789, France was torn apart by the French Revolution when radical democrats overthrew the country's monarchy. The leaders of the revolution and many ordinary French citizens now saw the Inquisition as an oppressive tool of the old regime, and they destroyed all of its remnants within French borders. The same thing happened on a larger scale during the Napoleonic Wars that occurred in the following decades. As French armies swept across much of Europe, the soldiers ransacked the Inquisition's prisons, chased away or killed the inquisitors, and captured or destroyed

The Inquisition temporarily shut down when Italy was invaded by Napoleon's troops.

thousands of the Inquisition's documents and records. When Napoleon's troops invaded Italy in 1796, the pope fled and the Inquisition was forced to temporarily shut down.

Permanently Eliminating the Inquisition

After the Napoleonic Wars, the Church reinstated the Holy Office. However, the Inquisition was no longer as powerful or fearsome as it was in the past. Clearly, it was no longer viable for the Church's agents to persecute, imprison, torture, and burn those who disagreed with traditional church doctrines. So, in 1826, the Church eliminated execution in the Inquisition. All prisoners then held in Inquisition jails were released and most of that institution's remaining documents were burned.

The Holy Office itself was not abolished, however. In fact, it still exists,

The duty proper to the Congregation for the Doctrine of the Faith is to promote and safeguard the doctrine on the faith and morals throughout the Catholic world. For this reason, everything which in any way touches such matter falls within its competence.[47]

Essentially, the mission of this remnant of the once-feared Inquisition is to promote and defend Catholic rules and ideas, particularly those dealing with subjects of a moral or ethical nature, such as abortion, euthanasia, and homosexuality.

Learning from the Inquisition

History has not forgotten the Inquisition. The fear and suffering spread by the Inquisition have left a lasting legacy in modern times. For example, both modern film and literature have attempted to

The Holy Office still exists as the Congregation for the Doctrine of the Faith. In 1988, Pope John Paul II defined its modern-day purpose.

albeit in a heavily altered form. In 1908 Pope Pius X changed its name to the Supreme Sacred Congregation of the Holy Office, and in 1965 Pope Paul VI changed it again to the Sacred Congregation for the Doctrine of the Faith. (The term Sacred was dropped later.) In 1988, Pope John Paul II defined the Congregation's purpose this way:

portray the violence and cruelty of the Inquisition as a message against religious intolerance. One such film is *The Name of the Rose*, an adaptation of the Umberto Eco novel of the same name. The film, made in 1986, features the story of a clergyman, played by Sean Connery, who challenged the Inquisition in Italy in the year 1327. In other art forms, there have been a number of modern plays that tell the story of Joan of Arc's trial and execution, and there is even an opera about Galileo.

The bigger question surrounding the Inquisition is: what can be learned from it? In reading and researching the Inquisition, one might come to an understanding that the brutality and violence of the Inquisition was a product of extreme religious zealotry and not devout religious faith. This understanding is often reached by Catholics, who have trouble reconciling the violent events of the Church's past with their own faith. Simply put, the actions of past Church leaders cannot be associated with the actions of current Church leaders. Or, As Baigent and Leigh wrote: "It would be a mistake … to identify the Inquisition with the Church as a whole. They are not the same institution. [The Inquisition] remains only one aspect of the Church" and its long history.[48]

In studying the Inquisition, one can also make conclusions about the nature of power, and the temptation of leaders to act unjustly when given too much authority. During the Inquisitions, inquisitors had the power to try, sentence, and even murder those whose beliefs were different from the teachings of the Church. This led to an abuse of power by Church leaders, and raises questions about the role of a central religious power in the personal lives of its followers.

Lastly, it is important to question whether the Inquisition was a "success." In modern times, it is difficult to think of an institution that tortured and murdered innocent people as "successful," but the Inquisition did have specific goals that it used these cruel methods to try and reach. Among these goals were: limiting other Christian movements, suppressing other religions, and halting the flow of new ideas. Looking back, one might conclude that even though it successfully destroyed the Cathars and Waldensians, the Inquisition did not prevent the spread of new ideas or new faiths. Protestantism grew in spite of the Inquisition, while Jews and Muslims simply relocated to countries where the Church was weak. In addition, victims such as Joan of Arc became martyrs at the hands of the Inquisition, and are now symbols of freedom in the face of intolerance. These failures of the Inquisition demonstrate the power of new ideas and the strength of the human spirit. The Inquisition could not truly silence the voices of those who opposed it, nor could it prevent people from practicing their beliefs.

Notes

Introduction: Contemporary Views on the Inquisition

1. Michael Baigent and Richard Leigh, *The Inquisition*. East Sussex, UK: Gardners, 2000, pp. xv–xvi.
2. Edward Peters, *Inquisition*. Berkeley, CA: University of California Press, 1989, p. 57.
3. Henry Kamen, *The Spanish Inquisition*. London, UK: White Lion, 1976, p. 284.
4. Quoted in Kamen, *Spanish Inquisition*, p. 286.
5. Ingram Cobbin, ed., *John Foxe's Book of Martyrs*. London, UK: Knight and Son, 1856, p. 1060.
6. Quoted in The *Catholic Encyclopedia for School and Home*. 12 vols. New York, NY: McGraw-Hill, 1965, vol. 5, p. 475.

Chapter One: The Birth of the Papal Inquisition

7. Quoted in Bernard Hamilton, The Medieval Inquisition. New York, NY: Holmes and Meier, 1981, p. 43.
8. Anne Fremantle, Age of Faith. New York, NY: Time, 1965, p. 12.
9. Louise Collis, Memoirs of a Medieval Woman: The Life and Times of Margery Kempe. New York, NY: Harper and Row, 1964, p. 11.
10. Quoted in Emmanuel Le Roy Ladurie, Montaillou. New York, NY: Vintage, 1975, pp. 78, 81.
11. Quoted in Jonathan Sumption, The Albigensian Crusade. London, UK: Faber and Faber, 1978, p. 93.
12. Quoted in Marie-Humbert Vicaire, St. Dominic and His Times. New York, NY: McGraw-Hill, 1964, p. 146.
13. Quoted in Henry C. Lea, A History of the Inquisition of the Middle Ages. 4 vols. New York, NY: Harbor Press, 1955, vol. 1, p. 329.
14. Quoted in Lea, History of the Inquisition, vol. 1, p. 329.
15. Baigent and Leigh, Inquisition, p. 28.
16. Baigent and Leigh, Inquisition, pp. 30–31.
17. Quoted in A.L. Maycock, The Inquisition. London, UK: Constable, p. 173.

Chapter Two:
The Politics of the
Medieval Inquisition

18. Quoted in Reinerius Saccho, "Of the Sects of the Modern Heretics." www.fordham.edu/halsall/source/waldo2.html

19. Quoted in Lea, History of the Inquisition, vol. 1, p. 296.

20. Baigent and Leigh, Inquisition, p. 48.

21. Quoted in Régine Pernoud, Joan of Arc: By Herself and Her Witnesses. Trans. Edward Hyams. Chelsea, MI: Scarborough House, 1994, p. 184.

22. Quoted in Wilfred T. Jewkes and Jerome B. Landfield, eds., Joan of Arc: Fact, Legend, and Literature. New York, NY: Harcourt, Brace and World, 1964, p. 78.

Chapter Three:
Roots and Objectives
of the Spanish Inquisition

23. Quoted in Rosemary Horrox, ed., The Black Death. Manchester, UK: Manchester University Press, 1994, p. 45.

24. Joseph Perez, The Spanish Inquisition. Trans. Janet Lloyd. New Haven, CT: Yale University Press, 2005, pp. 4–5.

25. Perez, Spanish Inquisition, p. 10.

26. Perez, Spanish Inquisition, p. 6.

27. Quoted in Paul J. Hauben, ed., The Spanish Inquisition: A Crucible of National Values. New York, NY: Wiley, 1969, p. 38.

28. Quoted in Baigent and Leigh, Inquisition, p. 63.

29. Quoted in Kamen, Spanish Inquisition, pp. 47–48.

30. Quoted in Kamen, Spanish Inquisition, p. 48.

Chapter Four:
Procedures and Penalties
of the Spanish Inquisition

31. Quoted in Kamen, Spanish Inquisition, p. 174.

32. Perez, Spanish Inquisition, p. 136.

33. Quoted in Kamen, Spanish Inquisition, pp. 165–166.

34. Quoted in Perez, Spanish Inquisition, p. 141.

35. Quoted in Perez, Spanish Inquisition, p. 147.

36. Baigent and Leigh, Inquisition, p. 71.

37. Quoted in Edward Burman, The Inquisition: The Hammer of Heresy. London, UK: Aquarius, 1984, p. 23.

38. Kamen, Spanish Inquisition, p. 185.

Chapter Five:
The Numerous Victims
of the Spanish Inquisition

39. Kamen, Spanish Inquisition, pp. 115– 116.

40. Perez, Spanish Inquisition, p. 62.

Chapter Six:
The New Inquisition and the Threat of Modern Science

41. Baigent and Leigh, Inquisition, p. 124.
42. Nicolaus Copernicus, On the Revolutions, trans. Edward Rosen. Baltimore, MD: Johns Hopkins University Press, 1992, p. 38.
43. Giordano Bruno, "The Ash Wednesday Supper," trans. Stanley L. Jaki. Dartmouth College, 1999, p. 7. hilbert.dartmouth.edu/~matc/Readers/renaissance.astro/6.1.Supper
44. Quoted in Giorgio de Santillana, The Crime of Galileo, Chicago, IL: The University of Chicago Press, 1955, p. 312.
45. Quoted in Giorgio de Santillana, The Crime of Galileo, p. 310.

Epilogue:
The Inquisition and Its Legacy

46. Quoted in John O'Brien, The Inquisition. New York, NY: Macmillan, 1973, p. 208.
47. Quoted in "Congregation for the Doctrine of the Faith." www.vatican.va/roman_curia/congregations/cfaith/documents/rc_con_cfaith_pro_14071997_en.html.
48. Baigent and Leigh, Inquisition, p. xv.

For More Information

Books

Baigent, Michael and Richard Leigh. *The Inquisition*. East Sussex, UK: Gardners, 2000.
Very well-researched, this is one of the best modern studies of all three of the main phases of the Inquisition.

Goldsmith, Mike. *Galileo Galilei*. New York, NY: Raintree/Steck Vaughn, 2002.
This book is a great presentation of Galileo's contributions to science and his famous run-in with the Inquisition for young readers.

Kamen, Henry. *The Spanish Inquisition: A Historical Revision*. New Haven, CT: Yale University Press, 2014.
This updated version of Kamen's research on the Spanish Inquisition is one of the greatest accomplishments of Inquisition scholarship and studies a wide range of topics, from how it started to how it ended, and everything in between.

Mayer, Thomas F. *The Roman Inquisition: A Papal Bureaucracy and its Laws in the Age of Galileo*. Philadelphia, PA: University of Pennsylvania Press, 2013.
An in-depth look at the Roman Inquisition, this book also investigates how the institution changed over time.

Murphy, Cullen. *God's Jury: The Inquisition and the Making of the Modern World*. Boston, MA: Houghton Mifflin Harcourt, 2012.
This book combines history and modern times, focusing on how the past Inquisitions can be influential to the present world.

White, Michael. *The Pope and the Heretic: The True Story of Giordano Bruno, the Man Who Dared to Defy the Roman Inquisition*. New York, NY: Harper Perennial, 2003.
Giordano Bruno was one of the most fascinating thinkers of the late Middle Ages and this study outlines his life and thought.

Websites

A Timeline of the Inquisitions
inquisition.library.nd.edu/timeline.RBSC-INQ:COLLECTION
This is a useful website, providing a detailed timeline of the various inquisitions from the papal Inquisition through the Spanish Inquisition.

The Templar Trials: Did the System Work?
www.usna.edu/Users/history/abels/crusades/gilmour-bryson-templartrials.pdf
This journal article examines the trials of the Templar Knights, and whether the practices and procedures were truly effective.

Joan of Arc
www.history.com/topics/saint-joan-of-arc
This website provides links to interesting topics from Joan of Arc's life, including informational and entertaining video clips and articles.

The Galileo Project
galileo.rice.edu/chr/inquisition.html
With an emphasis on the Roman Inquisition and Galileo, this site has general overviews and detailed descriptions of many Inquisition topics.

The Trial of Galileo
www.law.umkc.edu/faculty/projects/ftrials/galileo/galileo.html
This website has a useful collection of some of the main documents associated with Galileo's confrontation with the Inquisition.

Index

Templar Knights, 32–33
popes
    Boniface VIII, 27–28
    Cathars and, 18–19
    Clement V, 33
    Gregory IX, 6, 22–23
    Gregory X, 23
    Honorius III, 22
    Innocent III, 15, 18–20, 22, 30
    Innocent IV, 23
    Innocent VIII, 47
    John Paul II, 79, 87
    Julius III, Pope, 74
    kidnap of, 27–28
    luxurious lifestyle of, 30–31
    Paul III, 7, 73, 74
    Paul IV, 74
    Paul VI, 87
    Pius VII, 84–85
    Pius X, 87
    power struggles with secular
      leaders, 12, 17–18, 27, 46–47
    Sixtus IV, 45–47
    See also Catholic Church
Portugal, 42–43, 49
potro, 55
printing press, 72
prison, 24, 34–36, 46, 51–53, 55–57, 59,
  65, 69, 75, 81, 83, 85–86
property confiscation
    by medieval Inquisition, 13, 20,
      23–24, 33
    by Spanish Inquisition, 46, 51, 57,
      59
Protestants
    Black Legend and, 12–13
    discredit of Catholic Church, 13
    persecution of, 11–12
    propaganda in writings, 11
    Roman Inquisition and, 7, 72–74,
      85, 88
    Spanish Inquisition and, 39, 50,
      60, 66–70
pulley torture, 55

R
rack torture, 24, 54–55
Ramadan, 66
Reformation, 72–73
Roman Empire, 16, 24
Roman Inquisition
    early victims, 7, 74–75
    Holy Office and, 73, 75, 77-78,
      82-87
    knowledge control and, 72–75
    methods, 13–14
    overview, 72–73
    prominent individuals and, 75
    Reformation and, 72–73
    science and, 76–83
    Waldensians and, 74, 88

S
Saccho, Reinerius, 29
Sacred Congregation for the Doctrine
  of the Faith, 87
de Salazar, Alonso, 70
de San Martin, Juan, 45
de San Roman, Francisco, 69
Satan, 17

science
        Aristotle's view of universe, 76
        banned books, 7, 74, 77, 84
        heliocentric view of universe, 7,
            77, 79–81, 84–85
        Roman Inquisition and, 7, 14,
            76–83
        telescope, 80
        as threat to Catholic Church,
            76–83
Servet, Miguel, 69
Settele, Canon, 85
Sixtus VI, Pope, 45–47
social services, 17
sorcery, 24
soul, 17–19, 30, 35–36, 46, 48–49, 66
Spain
        administration of Spanish
            Inquisition, 6, 38–39, 45
        anti-Semitism, 39–41, 43, 45, 70
        control of inquisitors and, 12
        Jews expelled from, 6, 40, 44
        Muslims expelled from, 61–62, 66
        Waldensians in, 29
Spanish Inquisition
        administration of, 6, 38–39, 45
        anti-Semitism and, 39–41, 43, 45,
            70
        auto-da-fé, 57–59, 69
        backlash against, 46
        beatas and, 70–71
        bloodlines, 64
        conversos, 42–47, 60–61, 64–65, 68
        discredit of Spain and, 11–12
        Edict of Faith, 50–51, 66
        Edict of Grace, 70
        formal establishment of, 6, 45–47

        implications of heretics, 51–53
        methods, 13–14
        Muslims and, 8, 38, 50, 60, 64, 70,
            72
        organization, 49
        overview, 38–39
        property confiscation, 46, 51, 57,
            59
        Protestants and, 39, 50, 60, 66–70
        punishments, 56–57, 59
        purpose, 39–40, 42–43
        Suprema, 49, 51, 70
        torture and, 54–59
        trials, 51–52
        verdicts, 56–57, 59
        witchcraft, 70
strappado, 55
Suprema, 49, 51, 70
Switzerland, 69

T
Talmud, 74
telescope, 80
Templar Knights, 28, 32–34
theocracy, 18
toca, 55
de Torquemada, Tomás, 45, 46–47, 60
torture
        bloodshed and, 23–26
        as common, 13
        condoned by pope, 23
        confession and, 9–10, 24, 53
        in context of time period, 10–11
        elimination of use by Inquisition,
            86

Picture Credits

Cover Heritage Images/Contributor/Hulton Fine Art Collection/Getty Images; pp. 6-7 © iStockphoto.com/duncan1890; pp. 6 (left), 84 DEA/A. DAGLI ORTI/De Agostini Picture Library/Getty Images; pp. 6 (middle), 52 DEA/G. DAGLI ORTI/Contributor/De Agostini/Getty Images; pp. 6 (right), 74 Ipsumpix/Contributor/Corbis Historical/Getty Images; pp. 7 (left), 33 UniversalImagesGroup/Contributor/Universal Images Group/Getty Images; pp. 7 (right), 45 Courtesy of Wikimedia Commons; p. 9 Sala Frances, Emilio (1850-1910)/Prado, Madrid, Spain/Index/Bridgeman Images; p. 10 whitemay/E+/Getty Images; p. 12 Leemage/Contributor/Hulton Fine Art Collection/Getty Images; pp. 16, 19 PHAS/Contributor/Universal Images Group/Getty Images; p. 22 jorisvo/Shutterstock.com; p. 23 Leemage/Universal Images Group/Getty Images; pp. 25, 56 Culture Club/Contributor/Hulton Archive/Getty Images; p. 28 ZU_09/E+/Getty Images; p. 31 Archive Photos/Stringer/Archive Photos/Getty Images; p. 32 ullstein bild/Contributor/ullstein bild/Getty Images; p. 39 MPI/Stringer/Hulton Royals Collection/Getty Images; pp. 40, 82 Leemage/Contributor/Corbis Historical/Getty Images; p. 44 De Agostini/Biblioteca Ambrosiana/De Agostini Picture Library/Getty Images; p. 46 Popperfoto/Contributor/Popperfoto/Getty Images; p. 58 Stefano Bianchetti/Contributor/Corbis Historical/Getty Images; p. 61 Ken Welsh/Getty Images; p. 62 Pictures from History/Bridgeman Images; p. 63 Hulton Archive/Stringer/Hulton Archive/Getty Images; p. 67 Everett Historical/Shutterstock.com; p. 69 NLM/Science Source/Science Source/Getty Images; p. 73 Imagno/Hulton Archive/Getty Images; p. 75 Historical Picture Archive/Contributor/Corbis Historical/Getty Images; p. 78 Leemage/Contributor/Universal Images Group/Getty Images; p. 80 SHEILA TERRY/SCIENCE PHOTO LIBRARY/Science Photo Library/Getty Images; p. 86 Bibliotheque Nationale, Paris, France/Bridgeman Images; p. 87 giulio napolitano/Shutterstock.com.

About the Author

Kenneth Bartolotta is a lecturer of college writing at SUNY Buffalo State and an adjunct professor of English at Bryant & Stratton's Amherst Campus. A former journalist for various papers throughout Western New York, Mr. Bartolotta resides in West Seneca, NY.